VIRAL LEADERSHIP

SEIZE THE POWER OF NOW TO CREATE
LASTING TRANSFORMATION IN BUSINESS

DR. RICHARD K. NONGARD
WITH R.J. BANKS

www.RichardNongard.com | www.ViralLeadership.com

Viral Leadership:
Seize the Power of Now to Create Lasting Transformation in Business

Dr. Richard K. Nongard and R.J. Banks
Edited by Kelley T. Woods
Cover and Formatting by Rene Folsom

Copyright © 2018 by Dr. Richard K. Nongard and R.J. Banks. All Rights Reserved.

No part of this publication may be reproduced, stored in a retrieval system or transmitted in any form or by any means - electronic, mechanical, photocopy, recording or any other - without the prior written permission of the publisher. The only exception is brief quotations in printed reviews or scholarly journals.

First Printing: July 2018
ISBN-13: 978-1720404194 | ISBN-10: 1720404194

Dr. Richard K. Nongard
Peachtree Professional Education, Inc.
15560 N. Frank L. Wright Blvd. B4-118
Scottsdale, AZ 85260
(918) 236-6116

www.RichardNongard.com
www.ViralLeadership.com

ABOUT THE AUTHORS

Dr. Richard Nongard is a popular conference and keynote speaker, known for his relaxed and engaging style. His focus is on real-world solutions based on the science of leadership. His presentations focus on leadership, engagement and actionable strategies for business success. He holds a Doctorate in Transformational Leadership (Cultural Transformation) from Bakke Graduate University.

Richard is a business expert who started his career in 1983 as a cold-calling salesperson in the auto industry. With stints at both Nissan and Honda dealerships in the mid-1980s, he learned sales in the Zig-Ziglar style. Since then, he has engaged in both medical and educational sales, administration, and product development positions. Richard is a serial entrepreneur who has owned several restaurants along with a variety of successful business ventures over the years.

Richard is the author of numerous books, publications, and training videos. His first book on leadership,

Transformational Leadership: How to Lead from Your Strengths and Maximize Your Impact, has already become a popular resource for leadership development. He has written many other books as well, including psychology textbooks that have been adapted as textbooks at the university level, and his 5-star reviews are a testament to the value Richard provides in both written and spoken media.

Dr. Richard K. Nongard is a coach, consultant and lecturer, offering services to business groups, sales groups and healthcare organizations. You can bring him to your organization to train your executives or front-line employees in Viral Leadership, Appreciative Inquiry and/or Multiple Intelligences.

To bring Dr. Richard K. Nongard to your organization or conference as a keynote speaker contact him at www.RichardNongard.com or (918) 236-6116.

Robert (RJ) Banks is a lover of wisdom and a passionate student of life. He has discovered the true joy and happiness that arrives from serving and helping others by inspiring and empowering millions to live their greatest lives. Through his continued studies and experiences, he embodies and shares his knowledge and interpretation of inspired optimal living and co-creating the happy life we all deserve.

Having been taught the Law of Attraction at an early age, RJ has been blessed with an exciting and adventurous life! While proudly serving in the US Air Force, he was handpicked to join the USAF Thunderbirds air demonstration team. His post-military endeavors led him to Hollywood and the entertainment industry where he spent the next twelve years as a radio DJ, a recording studio owner, a music producer and professional musician. In his early forties, RJ further elevated his service to others by entering the medical field as a Diagnostic Imaging Specialist.

In 2013, RJ's life took an unexpected turn when he was diagnosed with an "inoperable" brain tumor. Within a very short time he had lost most everything in the material world. He could no longer work in radiology, he lost his six-figure income, his beautiful house at the local country club, all his fancy cars, his wife left, and he was told he only had 6 to 8 months to live. By using the power of the law of attraction,

RJ was blessed with finding a neurosurgeon who could perform the delicate brain surgery. Although the surgery was a success, RJ is now blind. But, he is also the happiest he has ever been in his life!

Through this challenge and leading up to his surgery, RJ became self-inspired and self-motivated to create his now famous LOA Affirmations audio programs. During this time, he wrote his bestselling book, *The Power of I Am and the Law of Attraction*. Within its pages, instead of using philosophical words explaining the meaning of the power of, "I AM" and the "Law of Attraction", he gives the reader practical steps on how to discover this natural power that is hidden within all of us. RJ reveals where to find it, how to develop and refine it and how to use it at will for whatever one truly desires.

After spending the next 4 years recovering from brain surgery and learning how to live as a blind person, RJ and his guide dog, Cabo, now reside in Las Vegas, Nevada, where he spends his time as a writer, a cognitive behavioral therapist, and a voice-over recording artist.

With over a half million followers on Facebook, (www.facebook.com/loaaffirmations), RJ is happily using and sharing his knowledge and experience with the power of the I AM and the Law of Attraction to help others break the cycle of being pulled and pushed by their own unknown commands of the Law of Attraction. He is currently in the final stages of completing his next book titled, *New Beginnings, and The Law of Attraction*, which details starting one's life over after experiencing sudden adversity.

Contact RJ at www.RobBanksVoiceovers.com

WHAT THE EXPERTS ARE SAYING ABOUT VIRAL LEADERSHIP

by Dr. Richard Nongard and RJ Banks

"Dr. Nongard shares great insights around viral leadership and how a simple idea, like our DoubleTree by Hilton cookie, can truly transform a business."

— Chris Nassetta, President & CEO, Hilton Worldwide Holdings, Inc.

"By activating each of the Four Quadrants of Viral Leadership identified in this book, you can step brilliantly into a new future. You will gain creative tools and find ways to innovate, build teams, organize around an idea or event, resulting in buy-in at every level for the vision – the key to creating lasting, long-term success."

— Randy Dobbs, Former CEO and President, GE Capital - Information Technology Solutions

"Viral Leadership has incredibly useful information and great stories to keep you motivated, and that's exactly what success is all about: getting, and staying, motivated. Growing up and being burdened with the mind of an entrepreneur by age 8, I would have loved to read a book like this in my teens, let alone as an adult. By using just a few simple principles, Richard Nongard and RJ Banks show us that all things are possible."

— Catherine Hickland, Television Personality on *One Life to Live* and *Knight Rider*, CEO of Cat Cosmetics

"Nongard & Banks share an outstanding balance of real-world experience and inspirational theory in Viral Leadership. The biggest takeaway is the value of connection. It's one thing to lead, it's another thing for your leadership go viral! You will discover how to inspire others to share your message as you read this book."

— Jason Linett, Speaker and Author of Work Smart Business

"Nongard and Banks are brilliant! I immediately took the ideas from this book straight to our team members to make sure we are capturing the moment and making something lasting out of our good ideas."

— Charles Horton, CEO of Fastbucks and the Firewalking Institute of Research and Education

"Do you want to inspire your teams to innovation and opportunity, and for this to become the new normal? Nongard & Banks show how to make this a reality in the pages of this book."

— Jill Greene, VP of Sales and Channel Partners, SafetySkills; Past President, Junior League of OKC

"Viral Leadership presents timely and relevant illustrations to help you transform your business and leverage your influence through common sense practices and today's technology platforms."

— Jeff Applegate, President and CEO, Texas Injection Molding, LLC

TABLE OF CONTENTS

Foreword 3
Part One
    Lasting Transformation through Viral Leadership 7
Chapter One
    Discover Your Cookie and Seize the Moment 9
Chapter Two
    Four Quadrants of Viral Leadership 21
Part Two
    Viral Leadership in Motion 31
Chapter Three
    Quadrant One: Creating Viral Teams 33
Chapter Four
    Quadrant Two: Innovative ideas 41
Chapter Five
    Quadrant Three: Ownership and Buy-In 51
Chapter Six
    Quadrant Four: Culture of Engagement 71
Part Three
    Foundations of Viral Leadership 81
Chapter Seven
    Foundation of Intention 83
Chapter Eight
    Viral Leadership is Built on Authenticity 93

Chapter Nine
Go V.I.R.A.L. 105

Part Four
Specific Ways to Activate Viral Leadership 115

Chapter Ten
How Intention Leads Us into Action 117

Chapter Eleven
Leadership for Everyone 129

Chapter Twelve
Lessons in Viral Leadership from Entertainment 139

Chapter Thirteen
Develop your Decisiveness 147

Epilogue
The Result is Lasting Transformation in Business 161

Chapter Fourteen
Activating the Power of Now 163

Dr. Richard K. Nongard and R.J. Banks

FOREWORD

I didn't enter the business world with the idea that I would ring the bell, but between the time I left Arkansas State University in 1972 and now, I have served at the officer level at the General Electric company and as CEO of General Electric Capital (Information Technology Solutions). I stemmed the net loss of $100 million a year from Operations, and within two years, the business had returned to a small profit of $12 million – an impressive swing in profitability of over $110 million on less than half the volume previously achieved. I was awarded the "Turnaround Business of the Year" by Jeff Immelt for the entirety of General Electric Company.

From GE I went on to hold the top position at Phillips Medical North America, US Investigation Services, Matrix Medical, and I currently mentor senior business leaders, serve as a board member on several boards, and provide various business services via my private consulting firm. My approach to leadership has been the approach of Transformational Leadership and, above all, I have emphasized authenticity. The turnaround at GE, my success at USIS and Matrix and my current roles on many boards, and my mentoring are predicated on the five hallmarks of Transformational Leadership – which I wrote about in my 2010 book,

Transformational Leadership: A Blueprint for Real Organizational Change.

Dr. Richard Nongard understands the value of Transformational Leadership, the importance of authenticity, and the steps needed to change a culture. In my book, I called this creating a cadre of leaders. In this book on Viral Leadership, Dr. Nongard shows how a model of Transformational Leadership can inspire leaders to access the power of the moment and step into long-term success by creating a legacy of related ideas, projects, and solutions that transform even more than expected. Nongard identifies how Viral Leadership spreads from one person and group to another, making owners, managers, employees, and the community stakeholders by generating buy-in and ownership of the leadership process along with an enthusiasm for the vision.

In this clearly written book, Dr. Nongard and R.J. Banks place their understanding of the Four Quadrants of Viral Leadership on top of a foundation of intention and authenticity. It is my belief that this foundation is a powerful key to success as a leader. An authentic leader is a powerful leader, not by might but through compassion. In my book I wrote that, "To truly succeed in the business world, to become an effective leader, to learn about yourself through your success and failures, you have to take risks. You have to put yourself in a position to really transform the business and transform yourself as a person. You have to get out of your comfort zone. You must ask for, take, and execute the hard jobs."

The authors of this book get it.

By activating each of the Four Quadrants of Viral Leadership identified in this book, you can step brilliantly into a new future. You will gain creative tools and find ways to innovate, build teams, organize around an idea or event, resulting in buy-in at every level for the vision – the key to creating lasting, long-term success.

Randy Dobbs
Greenville, SC
www.dobbsleadership.com

Author of *Transformational Leadership: A Blueprint for Real Organizational Change*

Former President and CEO, General Electric Capital, Information Technology Solutions

Former CEO USIS

Former CEO Matrix Medical

PART ONE

Lasting Transformation through Viral Leadership

CHAPTER ONE

Discover Your Cookie and Seize the Moment

Have you ever tasted one of those amazing delicious DoubleTree Hotel cookies? I am certain there are many other factors contributing to that hotel chain's success, but here is one observation that doesn't take a Harvard MBA to recognize: *These cookies are a huge part of the chain's success, and a great lesson in viral leadership.* You see, these always warm and fresh jewels of happiness have put smiles on the faces of over 500 million road-weary travelers since 1986. In fact, they did just that to me recently while I was in Houston or shall I say, while I was attempting to leave Houston. Let me explain.

I spend a great deal of time traveling throughout the country and even the world as a keynote speaker and executive coach. Hurriedly running from airports to hotels, to venues, engaging rental cars and typically, cold stale or vending machine food are normal fare for this lifestyle. But, this is my chosen path and it's also one that I love. On this trip, however, Murphy's Law was trying to get the best of me. The day had started out with amazing potential. I had a fantastic coaching call earlier in the morning, and my speaking engagement was a huge success with an enormous turnout. But to my dismay, my presentation went way too long, the crowd wanted more Q&A, and my already tight schedule was leaving me very little time, if any, to catch the last flight home.

While sitting in bumper to bumper traffic I found myself pondering over why and how things in my personal life had gotten so chaotic. I was behind on my emails, my daughter kept texting me from college with problems that were impossible for me to fix from 500 miles away and I knew that if I didn't get home that night my loving wife would be unhappy, and I was really dreading another lonely night in a hotel room. I had been on the road for weeks; I was tired, hungry, exhausted and just wanted to get home.

I remember the feeling of hopelessness and frustration as today of all days, TSA decided to add some icing to the cake, Murphy's cake, that is: As the alarms began screaming, "Beep-Beep-Beep-Beep," I knew my chances of being home in my wife's arms were looking dimmer and dimmer.

"Sir, your camera is giving me a positive," said the agent. And after a second screening and a top-secret discussion between the agent and supervisor, as well as a full and complete search of everything in, on and with me, I was finally given the green light. But, it was too late. As I watched my flight, the last flight of the night, pull away from the gate, I realized I was facing yet another lonely night in a hotel room.

Once the DoubleTree Airport shuttle dropped me off at the hotel's entrance, I became aware of the pangs of hunger I had ignored all afternoon. Combine a little frustration with pangs of hunger and it is easy to lose sight of the many things in one's life to be grateful for. While at the front desk checking in, I realized my mouth was watering like Pavlov's dog and my senses were delighted with the familiar smell of those ever so famous and always delicious DoubleTree Cookies. I walked quickly to my room, the fresh, hot cinnamon and chocolate cookies now in my possession. I knew I would be eating dessert before getting my supper! I still remember sitting on my bed, talking to my wife, and stuffing my face with those cookies. She had a great spirit about her, as always, and assured me that all is well and that she still loved me. I paused, mumbling half-honestly, "At least I have cookies to make me a little bit happier tonight."

As I ate the last crumbs from the wrapper, I texted my daughter. I kicked off my shoes. I dialed room service for some real dinner, and all was good again, thanks to these amazing DoubleTree cookies.

While relaxing and finishing my dinner, I started thinking about how this whole DoubleTree cookie thing got started. I imagined a fluffy, warmhearted story about a DoubleTree desk clerk passionately sharing her grandmother's homemade cookies with her exhausted guests as they checked in. But after a quick internet search, it appears the whole cookie idea, which is as prevalent to business travelers as cat memes are to social media, was carefully planned. The idea was most likely conceived in a meeting, to build brand loyalty through a nightly turn-down service, and it worked! The DoubleTree brand is, and has been, the fastest growing hotel chain for the Hilton Corporation for over 10 years and is still growing.

That evening in Houston really sparked my curiosity and intrigue about success. My business brain needed to get to the root of this genius marketing strategy. So later that week, once I returned to my happy home and family, I reached out to the DoubleTree public relations and marketing team to discover the real origin of their delicious cookies. I must admit a tad of disappointment when I found out there was no famous desk clerk who shared her grandmother's cookies. It was a strategic marketing decision, one that was such a simple yet extremely effective gesture of caring which became so popular, so effective, that every DoubleTree in the world now bakes these legendary cookies onsite! Once out of the oven, they are placed in a warming box at the front desk, illustrating and reiterating the brand's welcoming and caring service. I even found them in Beijing last year at the DoubleTree and even though it was my first trip to China and I was excited by new possibilities and a different culture, these cookies made me feel right at home.

How does giving away half-a-billion cookies make DoubleTree a forerunner in Viral Leadership? Is a cookie leadership? No, a cookie is a gimmick, but this cookie has not crumbled in over 35 years! This is amazing sustainability and effective marketing and it tells us that something good has been cooking at Doubletree by Hilton: Leadership, Viral Leadership!

Much like the DoubleTree cookie concept, Viral Leadership can be lasting and create a legacy of related ideas, projects, and solutions. These innovative ideas are often sustainable and can even transform far beyond their original purpose. And of course, within the cookie story exists such a transformational idea. After almost 30 years since its conception, the DoubleTree cookie has now transitioned into the 21st century and internet era, even bigger and more famous than ever. A quick Google search finds 22 pages of websites centering on the cookie. There are cooking website devoted to replicating its amazing taste, several social media discussions organized around the cookie, including a website and Facebook page dedicated just to that cookie!

Do not mistake Viral Leadership for a flash in the pan or flavor of the month type of leadership. When the cookie was introduced back in 1989, I was in college. Now I am in my 50s and I still choose the DoubleTree by Hilton as my default, "go to" hotel. Why? Because I know exactly what I will get, and as simple as the cookies are, that type of consistency fueled a small chain of 25 hotels into what is now one of Hilton's most successful brands.

Is there unity around the cookie? Yes, there is. Because leadership that is effective is leadership that is unifying. It spreads from one person or group to another and commonly bonds everyone involved. This practice turns the hotel owners, managers, employees and even the community into stakeholders of a cookie empire by generating buy-in and ownership of the leadership process and an enthusiasm for the vision. How can this affect a community, you may ask? By getting and staying involved with the community:

To date, more than 1,250,000 chocolate chip cookies have been donated to members of the community from doctors and nurses, police and firefighters, as well as non-profit groups such as food banks and homeless shelters. During the 2016 and 2017 winter holiday seasons, the brand also celebrated 12 Days of Cookies - a welcoming invitation to both guests and non-guests - to stop into any U.S. DoubleTree location and pick up the brand's signature DoubleTree Cookie to save for Santa or, enjoy themselves.

"Going viral", in the vocabulary of the modern internet and mass media, refers to anything that unexpectedly and enthusiastically catches the attention of millions of people. It can be a story, a meme (those odd pictures with captions that get reposted over and over), a product, an idea or even a news story. The viral phenomena may be positive and socially redeeming, or it can be negative or even morally bankrupt. Some of these are funny and some are more serious in nature. The common denominator is that they quickly catch people's attention and the recipient is then (self) motivated to share it with others. This is how a father, who posts something hilarious with his kid on YouTube, can suddenly garner millions of views. For example, the *"David after Dentist"* video now has over 137 million views. This video alone has generated enough money for the family to pay tuition for private school for both David and his brother.

Even before the internet, things went viral. Commercial lines like, "Where's the beef?!" become cultural phenomena. That line from a Wendy's commercial even made it into the 1984 presidential debate punch lines and was repeated everywhere as it became part of the cultural lexicon of the 1980s. And, of course, the hula-hoop craze is an example of a product going viral, with 25 million being sold in the first four months after Wham-O introduced them in 1958. A more modern example of the viral obsession is the Pokemon phenomenon. Starting as a Gameboy game in 1996 (a portable handheld game console), within 2 years they advanced to the bigger Nintendo 64 home game console. This led to Pokemon Trading Cards in 2000, thus developing further into a Pokemon TV channel, Pokemon movies, and Pokemon merchandizing. In 2016, twenty years after its original conception, the developers recaptured their original fan base, plus an entirely new generation, with Pokemon Go. The game utilizes the player's cell phone GPS ability to locate, capture, battle, and train virtual creatures in the "real world." You may recall the viral craze as people of all ages were running around town "capturing" Pokemon characters. To date, the Pokemon franchise is said to be worth around 15 billion dollars.

Viral ideas, inventions, songs, and images, whether their viral fame comes from the internet or through other forms of recognition, is remarkable. But explosive or temporary fame, the proverbial 15-minutes of fame, is not enough to create a sustaining change. If something catches the momentum of the moment, it is leadership that will create the transformation and successful sustainability.

In 2012, Lydia Callis was selected as the sign-language interpreter for the deaf community as New York prepared for Hurricane Sandy. During the press conference the contrast between the dry-speaking monotones of Mayor Michael Bloomberg, who articulated "just the facts", was in stark contrast with the animated and passionate ASL signer. This legendary broadcast has now garnered millions of video views. She trended on Twitter. John Steward featured her press conference on "The Daily Show" and within a week, Saturday Night Live spoofed her role as the provider of information to the deaf community. It wasn't just New Yorkers who were amazed by her skill and entertained by her enthusiasm, it was now the entire country!

Lydia Callis was no flash in the pan. Although her fame only lasted 15 minutes, she seized the momentum of the moment. She intuitively understood the power of her viral phenomena and took advantage of the opportunity. She resigned her position in the Mayor's office and started her own company: LC Interpreting Services. "Interpreting is my calling," she enthusiastically boasts. It is very apparent that she loves what she does. Her Viral Leadership has created a lasting impact that goes beyond the immediate clients she works with. Lydia and her company now provides training in cultural competency, interpreter mentoring and ASL training for individuals and organizations around the world. Because of her impact that day and the resulting viral momentum she created, signing, which was once a rarity in informational media, now is considered an essential component of emergency communication and has been used coast-to-coast as a direct result of her influence and advocacy.

Yes, viral trends did give us "eating Tide pods" and "Elf Yourself" but it also gave us people like Lydia Callis. To see the lasting results of her work makes you feel pretty good, doesn't it? Fortunately, for every silly viral phenomena that has emerged, there seems to be an infinite list of positive phenomena. TED Talks, which had educated people around the globe, is a viral phenomenon, and long ago reached its billionth view.

Viral phenomena, coupled with effective leadership, has created sustainable fundraising campaigns for illnesses such as ALS (Lou Gehrig's disease) through the Ice Bucket Challenge. This viral sensation has included participants from presidents to celebrities and everyday people with a cellphone camera and a bucket full of ice. Yes, it was fun, entertaining and raised over 150 million dollars, but the real miracle, as a direct result of the challenge and the monies it generated, was the discovery of a gene that is the cause of the disease. Pat Quinn, who had lost his ability to speak due to ALS, was one of the original founders of the Ice Bucket Challenge. As a touching example of good karma, Pat has now regained his voice due to advancements that, in part, were funded by the monies he helped raise through the Ice Bucket challenge.

Viral Leadership – Mary Barra at GM Found Her Cookie

Mary Barra knows how to seize the moment and has created lasting fame not only for her leadership, but also for General Motors. Later in this book I share some of the leadership attributes of Alan Mullaly, the former Ford Motor Company CEO who took over the reins in the mid-2000s when General Motors and Chrysler were in bankruptcy. What he did then was to steer Ford in a remarkable direction by making the whole company a Viral Team. But Mary Barra took over the reins of GM in 2014 and serves as the current CEO. Her leadership and tenure are as remarkable as Mullaly's leadership and sales, innovation and change at GM puts her on track to be one of those innovative and influential Viral Leaders in history. Leading GM to a point where it is succeeding at what Tesla is only still promising, Barra has created an organization that excels at every level in technology, customer satisfaction, profit making and has even emerged as a technology leader in self-driving technology and artificial intelligence. You can say she has found her cookie for GM, and that cookie is mass-produced electric cars that are affordable to the masses.

Barra's leadership goes beyond her role at GM; she has called for more women to pursue STEM degrees and take leadership roles in business. In a report that she co-authored with Linamar CEO Linda Hasenfratz, she wrote, "If half the population is not playing its full role in ground-breaking fields such as artificial intelligence, self-driving vehicles, advanced materials and 3D printing, we face a grave risk of debilitating labor shortages and, as a result, slower growth for the entire economy."

Mary Barra recognized that we are at a unique time, where technology is driving culture, and investing in innovation can bring even a company that a decade ago was lagging, into viral success. The Chevy Bolt EV batteries currently outlast a Tesla battery and GM has acquired technology leaders, Cruise Automation, to position the Bolt in the forefront of driverless technology. But the most important question is: are customers happy? In 2016 GM enjoyed enormous sales growth and can boast the number one selling pure-electric car.

As a leader, Barra faced crisis head on, altering the company culture at GM by firing more than half a dozen executives following an ignition switch recall that had led to 124 deaths. She took ownership of the problems at GM and honored her promise to correct problems she inherited by making safety a genuine priority, along with implanting systems to flag new problems early on. But above all, Barra has seized the moment – by investing heavily in emerging technology and fostering a sincere desire to create the best products on the market.

Viral Leadership harnesses the momentum of the moment, transforming that awareness, enthusiasm, and excitement into something meaningful and lasting. Viral Leadership changes lives and transforms the moment into something sustainable. Pat Quinn did it, Lydia Callis did it, Mary Barra did it, and you, too, can be the leader who does it for your organization.

CHAPTER TWO

Four Quadrants of Viral Leadership

Viral Leadership emerges quickly and at any level within an organization. It can be organic and spontaneous or intentional and directed. Viral Leadership can be lasting and can create a legacy of related ideas, projects, and solutions that transform even more than expected. It spreads from one person and group to another; making owners, managers, employees and the community all stakeholders by generating buy-in and ownership of the leadership process, along with enthusiasm for the vision.

There are two distinct themes you are going to notice throughout this book. First, that *business is perhaps one of the most magnificent creations of all time*. And second, *that effective leadership is viral in nature*. Viral Leadership ignites others, it creates innovation, and it continues to build upon itself. It creates a culture of engagement, not just among the executive, but at every level.

For more than a decade *synergy* was the buzzword in business training programs. Synergy is defined as: *The interaction or cooperation of two or more organizations, substances, or other agents to produce a combined effect greater than the sum of their separate effects.* Viral Leadership is the synergetic type of leadership that brings stakeholders togethers, transcends hierarchy, and allows leverage between divisions and resources. As a result, Viral Leadership creates a sustaining air of contentment and happiness, allowing all parties have a sense of self-satisfaction, contentment, self-worth and generativity. There is perhaps nothing more satisfying than being both secure in the lasting value of leadership and benefitting from the significance of your efforts.

There have been countless career survey group studies over the years that consistently reveal the number one reason most people are dissatisfied, unhappy and often leave the company: That reason is because of a lack of recognition. Richard Eggleston, a top executive recruiter for the Morgan McKinley Group, agrees that one of the most frustrating aspects of any job is feeling unrecognized.

In my previous book on leadership I wrote, "The heart of Transformational Leadership is to transform others while transforming one's self." You have undoubtedly come to this book to either enhance your leadership abilities or to begin developing yourself as a leader. Whichever the reason or motive, your starting point begins with transforming yourself. This occurs by learning not only about leadership, but also learning how to seize the power of Now to create lasting transformation in business. The concepts in this book reach far beyond business applications. You will soon realize that once you enhance your business leadership acumen, you will find yourself becoming a more effective family member, community member and citizen of the world.

Viral Leadership, at its core, is about people and about relationships. It's not about doing something to people but doing something with people. Viral Leadership is collaborative and joins with others, rather than intimidating others by directing them through negative motivation.

Viral Leadership is a true form of synergistic leadership, in which motivation to action comes from the leader's own growth and enthusiasm and then spreads throughout an organization. This synergy is ripe with new possibilities. Viral Leadership is a dynamic leadership that recognizes change as a constant and that as a result, leadership is an ongoing function of organizational and individual wellness. Viral Leadership utilizes processes that have shown efficacy to create lasting changes in individuals, communities, organizations, and even in the world.

Why do you want to learn more about leadership? What is it that you are trying to transform or develop within yourself? Take a moment right now and clarify your motives. You have come to these pages on a quest to learn more and to enhance your success as a leader. Knowing your reasons 'why' will help keep you focused and motivated. Progress, growth and innovation are all propagated through Viral Leadership. Knowing why, where and how you fit in provides a very sturdy foundation to build upon. The when is, of course, NOW!

The Doorway to the Four Quadrants of Viral Leadership

We begin now at the doorway to the Four Quadrants of Viral Leadership. In recognizing the reasons to become a better leader, we begin to access these four quadrants. There is an infinite list of reasons driving desire to improve leadership performance. At a basic level, leadership creates security and significance, which are the two primary components of lasting happiness, according to author Robert McGee.

Some people might want to enhance their efficacy as leaders because they have become bored or stagnant in their current business. Others may want to enhance their leadership to take advantage of something that perhaps is yet unknown (changing technology), while yet others study leadership so they can emulate the great successes of previous leaders. An entire industry of historians who study presidential leadership exists; some of the best-selling business books have been of the "How I led a company to success" genre (think of bestselling author and CEO, Lee Iacocca, and Jack Welch who wrote, *Winning: The Ultimate Business How-To Book*).

You are now ready for action and to open the door to the infinite possibilities of transformation that can come from mastering viral leadership! Let's move forward into the Four Quadrants of Viral Leadership.

In creating this book, we have spent countless hours looking at our own experiences managing people and projects. Rob Banks has been a healthcare executive and an entertainment industry executive, and Richard Nongard has been both an educational services CEO an independent businessman. Through numerous discussions, based on our academic knowledge and personal experiences, we have found that Viral Leadership develops, and creates, from within a clearly identified set of quadrants.

To some extent this can be a linear process, moving from the first step through the fourth step. Idealistically, this linear structure can help conceptualize moving forward. This linear vantage point gives us a clear pathway to proceed with the rest of our learnings but, bear in mind, not only do authenticity and intention undergird every aspect of Viral Leadership, elements of Viral Leadership can overlap, coexist, and be repeated at different levels and through multiple transformations. In our configuration, parts of each quadrant may be accessed at any time. Sometimes there is overlap in the workings of each. These four elements are built upon the essential foundation of authenticity and intention.

The Four Quadrants of Viral Leadership include:

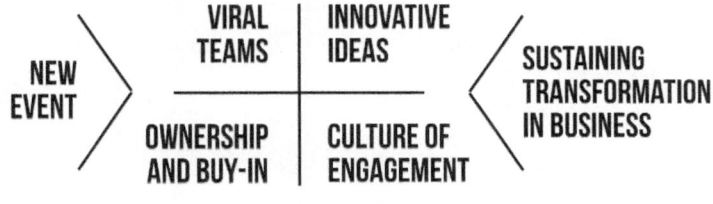

We begin our quest as a viral leader at creating a Viral Team. There is no such thing as leadership without others to lead. Although it is possible to hold an executive title or position without engaging others, this is not leadership. The history of business is filled with companies led by innovative founders or executives who refused to engage others. This is often out of proprietary fears, pride or narcissism. These businesses will not be case studies in this book because in almost every case, they failed. Ken Lay, the CEO of Enron, John Rigas at Adelphia Communications, and Bernard Ebbers at WorldCom are all examples of how authoritarian or totalitarian leadership can also become a fiasco that bankrupts stakeholders and destroys lives. Leadership of any kind only exists with others - there must be followers. In the case of Viral Leadership, people create the vision as a group or team. Otherwise, it is not leadership and, as we have learned, is then instead a spectacle of failure often riddled with greed, ego and corruption.

Viral Leadership is dynamic and moves to innovative ideas. These ideas can be organic, emerging unexpectedly as opportunities to be taken advantage of. Currently we often see this in the technology fields as companies and innovations evolve. These can come in the form of spectacular inventions that revolutionize society and create viral adaptation. Apple's Fitbit and Siri, Amazon's Alexa, and Google's AI assistant are all great examples of current viral innovations.

Viral innovation happens at all levels and within any industry. Viral innovation can refer to the assembly line in manufacturing, block chaining in financial service companies, virtual reality in the entertainment and psychology industries. Viral innovation can also be found in everyday products from new drinks (Red Bull) to new fads like fidget spinners. Ty Inc., a stuffed toy company, spun viral success into a sustaining legacy starting back in 1986. A few years later, in 1993, they created a viral frenzy with Beanie Babies. Their legacy still lives on to this day. In fact, today on eBay I was amazed to see the Beanie Baby "Princess Bear" selling for $500,000! Talk about a ROI on a $10 toy! This past week my adult daughter came to visit after graduating from college. She brought with her a gift of a Ty plush toy for her nine-year old step sister. This is 25 years after the Beanie Baby craze began, the same year my daughter was born.

On the opposite side of the Viral Leadership coin is that viral innovative ideas can be planned and structured. In this context the epicenter of Viral Leadership can be directed, planned and sought after.

Zappos.com, a popular online shoe store, is a great example of a company intending to create viral customer service in the already existing competitive shoe market. The Coca-Cola Company is another strong model of planned viral innovation and leadership. After over 126 years in business, they continue to create new markets through innovative ways of introducing their product to the next generation.

Innovation, in and of itself, is not enough for true success. Viral Leadership must be implemented to explore and consider every possibility. There is an ancient Chinese proverb describing how one thousand candles can be lighted from the flame of just one candle, and the life of the candle will not be shortened. Viral Leadership begins with you: the flame of that one single candle. Viral Leadership must then spread and transform others by training team members and allowing them judgement-free opportunities and environments. This creates a very positive and dynamic work environment as well as buy-in at all levels. This one single adjustment in you, the Viral Leader, is the starting point. This action soon multiplies success with team ownership of ideas, vision and the opportunity for every stakeholder in the organization to contribute.

The result becomes a perpetual motion machine of Viral Leadership, inspiring a culture of innovation, and excitement. It motivates others to achieve a higher level of worthiness, success and career contentment. This is the wonderful thing about Viral Leadership.

Not everybody can or should be a boss, but everyone can be a leader! A basis of esprit de corps, mentoring and engagement is the true foundational environment to strive for. Viral Leadership moves to a point where people no longer say, "It's not my job" or "As soon as I get a better offer, I'm out of here!" By providing truly nonjudgmental opportunities and an opportunistic environment you will soon start to hear things like, "I love being a part of what we are doing!" This is the result of synergetic Viral Leadership!

This is in part the beauty of Viral Leadership - because it is so sustaining, it also allows for multiple transformations where change can be successfully handled. The world is an ever-changing place. When Coca-Cola was first introduced in the 1800s we had just endured the Civil War. We did not have cars, we did not have telephones, and we certainly did not have the technology we have today. The Coca-Cola Company has sustained and adapted to every generation for over 126 years with a foundation of authenticity. IBM evolved products from punch card readers in 1911 into the personal computing era of the 1990s (is your computer IBM compatible?).

The doorway through which you entered Viral Leadership leads to a new paradigm of sustaining results. To some extent you can also view this as entering the doorway of self-recognition. The best place to start at becoming an effective Viral Leader requires self-evaluation and transformation. By meeting your deepest needs and then mastering each of the Four Quadrants we outline, you will be on your way to the ultimate Viral Leadership goal: creating and sustaining a lasting transformation in business. We do not study Viral Leadership because something needs to change, but because things are always changing. Now, let's open the door to the First Quadrant and start creating Viral Teams.

PART TWO

Viral Leadership in Motion

CHAPTER THREE

Quadrant One: Creating Viral Teams

I am confident that most everyone reading this book has either owned, rented or at least ridden in a Ford Taurus. Spanning 3 decades (1986 to present) and with over 8 million cars sold, the Ford Taurus is an American icon. As one of the best-selling cars in history, one can safely say that it has sold so well, that it became viral.

    I once owned a 2001 Taurus. I remember buying it and thinking it was the most average car I ever owned. But, I needed a comfortable and inexpensive car since, at that time, I was racking up the miles doing keynote speeches and trainings all over Texas and the Southwest. In one week I could easily drive a couple of thousand miles driving between Houston and Lubbock and then returning to my base in Wichita. I also recall eating more than my fair share of DoubleTree cookies while on the road in my dandy Taurus during my routine eight-hour drive home every Friday evening!

    Have you considered purchasing a new car within the last 5 or so years? No matter which model, I'm sure you have contemplated buying a shiny new Ford. They've offered great value, style and reliability for many years. However, had I asked you this same question 12 years ago, amid massive recalls, arbitration dealer closings and teetering on financial collapse, Ford probably wasn't in the running. So, what made the difference between the strong and successful Ford Motor Company of today and the failing company that was dying on the vine? The answer: Viral Leadership.

Throughout the 1980s and 1990s, the Taurus was everywhere. It was the bestselling car in America in the early 1990s, but by the time I bought my football-shaped Taurus, it was no longer a car one picked to buy, but a car that picked you because of incentives, price point or utility. It certainly wasn't the car of one's dreams. I ended up giving the car to my teenage son in 2006 when he was turning 16 and learning to drive. He finished it off within the first year.

At around the same time I was handing the Taurus keys over to my son, something amazing was happening in Detroit. CEO William C. Ford III found hope for his flailing company and its over 200 thousand hard-working employees. What he had found was a new CEO, one who was not from the auto industry. He was an aeronautical engineer named Alan Mulally and, as it turned out, he was a Viral Leader who understood the power of Now along with the value of Viral Team building.

The First Quadrant of Viral Leadership is Viral Team building, and Alan Mulally is going down in CEO history as one who was able to create a Viral Team, working in unison and sharing his vision. His teams included every level of employee and stakeholder.

On his first day as CEO, Mulally set out to see the product lineup and the first thing he asked was, "Where is the Taurus?" The other executives pointed out that they had killed the Taurus after the recent football-shaped models flopped. They had assumed the Taurus brand had run its course and it was time to move on to something new.

Although Mr. Mulally understood the value of branding, more importantly he understood that things reach a critical mass and with the right decisions can be sustainable. He also understood the power of Now. Just prior to his taking over as CEO, the Ford Company had reintroduced the 500 brand name off the Galaxy 500 brand from the 60s & 70s. The 500 was never as well known as the Taurus, nor did it ever establish brand loyalty, especially those models in the 1990s. My step-father had owned nothing but Tauruses in the 1980s and 1990s and while people wanted to love the car, they just didn't want the unreliability of the current car.

As the new leader of Ford, Mulally's first directive was simple: "'You've got until tomorrow to find a vehicle to put the Taurus name on because that's why I'm here. Then you have two years to make the coolest vehicle that you can possibly make." This aspect of the story of Ford's transformation is probably as important as anything else. Mulally understood that the only moment we have is right now and demanded instant action on what he perceived as a poor decision. He didn't second guess, he didn't hold a meeting on it, he made the decision and lived in the moment.

Viral Leadership is about knowing when to improve something rather than change something. Viral Leadership is about taking the momentum of a product or service and going deep rather than giving up. Although the Taurus never regained its sales momentum, it was used wisely by Ford as a showcase for emerging technology, and Mulally's vision as a "mobility company" partnered with communication and entertainment companies to make the mobile communication experience cutting-edge, exclusive at that time to Ford vehicles.

Another famous Mulally quote occurred when he was asked about being open to a merger. His reply, "Yes! We're going to merge with ourselves." The action he took was to create "One Ford" out of the fragmented division that in many cases, did not cooperate or coordinate. This included Ford of Asia, Ford of Europe, other divisions around the USA and around the world. The result: "One Ford" - a company with more horsepower than a turbo charged 428 Cobra Jet engine! What Mullally was doing from early on was creating Viral Teams while gaining the buy-in for the vision of a unified company.

Mulally's tenure was filled with great decisions. Undoubtedly, he was a deliberate leader who was able to weigh each corporate option with the precision only a rocket scientist could do. He was the only American car manufacturing company executive who turned down government bailout money and did not lead his company into bankruptcy. Mulally understood that government money always came with strings attached and he clearly had a different set of strings to play.

Although he has been hailed for his strategic leadership and business insight, it was his ability to be a transformational leader that truly predicated the change at Ford Motor Company. In fact, a testament to the viral nature of his leadership is that over the years numerous business books, journals and magazine articles highlighting successful leadership look at his tenure at Ford and leadership style as something to emulate. A whole generation of new business leaders in MBA programs are studying exactly what separated Mullaly from other, not so successful CEOs and company leaders.

Mullaly embraced leadership as a privilege that encompassed positive vantage points. He was not hung up on what was wrong with the Taurus but focused on what was right with the brand. Intentional or not, his appreciative nature was a signature of his leadership. He wrote:

"At the most fundamental level, it is an honor to serve — at whatever type or size of organization you are privileged to lead, whether it is a for-profit or nonprofit. It is an honor to serve. Starting from that foundation, it is important to have a compelling vision and a comprehensive plan. Positive leadership—conveying the idea that there is always a way forward — is so important, because that is what you are here for — to figure out how to move the organization forward. Critical to doing that is reinforcing the idea that everyone is included. Everyone is part of the team and everyone's contribution is respected, so everyone should participate."

Mr. Mulally's visions and beliefs in this statement, are the quintessence of Viral Leadership and reminds me of another viral leader: Sir Richard Branson. Here are a couple of quotes from him that display his Viral Leadership philosophy:

"Creating a business that really listens to its people is of paramount importance. Happy and thriving people make a happy and thriving business, which throughout my career has proven the best formula for success."

And, *"Take care of your employees, they will take care of your business."*

These quotes speak volumes about Viral Team building at every level. Employee loyalty, devotion and "buy-in" is a hallmark of Viral Leadership. Mulally and Branson both understand that viral success is grounded on everyone being a part of the team.

For Mulally to restore the car company, he focused on four things:

Creating a team who was virally enthusiastic about being a part of the solution. (Quadrant One)

On the business side he knew the viral possibilities of leveraged global assets and brought all divisions under one Ford – he re-innovated the business structure. (Quadrant Two)

Building cars that enthused customers, and creating ownership and buy-in. (Quadrant Three)

Creating a sustainable financing plan, without reliance on Uncle Sam. This changed the culture forever. (Quadrant Four)

Under the command of their new leader, Mulally required everyone at Ford become a team member. From the assembly workers to the executives, and from the dealer network to the financing team, everyone, no matter what the position or title they held, was equally "invested" in the success of the company. This is a hallmark of Viral Leadership, creating loyalty and genuine concern for the overall success of the company. This team "buy-in", or dedicated commitment, creates company-wide support at all levels, both vertically and horizontally rather than preserving egos, bonuses or status.

When I was working on my doctorate in leadership, one of my mentors, Dr. Lloyd Bakke, asked me, "How can we come alongside of you and support you?" In fact, of all the things I learned about leadership in academia, this one line - a sincere question from Lloyd as I persevered through the doctoral process - has stuck with me more than perhaps any other lesson I had in a classroom. And this is what Mulally did to change the toxic culture of Ford, and what you can do to create viral enthusiasm and buy-in from every stakeholder in your organization.

CHAPTER FOUR

Quadrant Two: Innovative ideas

The Second Quadrant of Viral Leadership addresses innovative ideas. In 2006, I had my own viral success experience we can attribute to the innovative idea of YouTube. It all started when I called out for my son, "Ricky, I need you to help me move a bookcase in the office!" But I got no answer. I knew he was home, he didn't tell me of any plans and being too young to drive, he couldn't have gone anywhere. At that time, I was living in Andover, Kansas. Andover is just east of Wichita and there really wasn't anywhere to go anyway. "Ricky!" I called out again, "Come help me." Still no reply.

As any parent of a teenager knows and understands, I had to go look for him. He wasn't in the kitchen and he wasn't in his bedroom. Finally, I opened the front door, and there he was, laying in the grass with a can of spray paint in his hand, screaming about the ozone layer. A camera was set on a tripod and I disrupted his concentration when I called out, "Ricky, what on Earth are you doing?!" "Dad," he said, "I'm making a video. There is a new thing on the internet called YouTube and I want to make a video and a lot of people will watch it."

"Ricky, I have work to do, and I need you to help me move a bookcase in the office."

"Okay, Dad. I'll be there in a minute."

I walked back into the house and to my office and waited. It sure seemed longer than a minute. Finally, Ricky showed up, sensing my impatience and, probably as a move to save his own hide, he blurted out, "You make videos, Dad, do you want me to help you put them on YouTube?"

I had never been to the YouTube website before this, and the desktop computer was on. He quickly sat in my chair, showed me YouTube and encouraged me, "Put one of your videos up!"

I told him, "That is for kids, and I don't do anything silly in my videos."

At that time, I owned a company that produced training resources for other mental health professionals and my videos consisted of teaching segments for counselors and therapists. "Nobody will watch my videos" I said, "They are just for therapists."

But, like, father, like son: Ricky's passion and tenacity convinced me to have a look at this silly YouTube fad. We sat together at my computer for the next hour and looked through the videos I had from my classes. By the end of the day we had uploaded a simple video of me guiding a class through a relaxation and stress management exercise. By morning, the video had almost 100 views and I was amazed. In time there were 1000 hits and I was shocked. Soon, the video seemed to take on a life of its own and eventually hit 10,000 viewers, and then 100,000 viewers! When it cracked half a million, I was not only grateful to my son for teaching me about YouTube, I was watching my other videos gain tens of thousands of hits. And yes, eventually that original posted video got over a million views.

But more importantly than views, it gave me a connection - connection at first to the YouTube community, but then to the people who benefitted from my videos who sent me emails, messages and even looked up my phone number and called me. After years of toiling day-to-day as a therapist who trained other therapists, I was now an internationally-known therapist, and I subsequently created an international organization for other professionals, sharing with them the same techniques in worldwide classes that I was previously limited to sharing locally with other professionals. I traveled to Manchester, UK and Canada, and coast-to-coast in the USA, discovering that viral content created connection.

My and Ricky's little YouTube adventure that day, uploading that first video, resulted in the formation of an international professional organization that I preside over. We now have over 5500 members worldwide and a cadre of leaders. Our leaders are highly trained to help others under the umbrella of the content that was in that first video.

Innovation takes us beyond our initial goals, and Viral Leadership allows us to experience creative energy, which is a catalyst for lasting transformation. I look back to that first YouTube video and attribute that first share in 2006 to a note I got today from one of our organizational leaders, thanking me for teaching him how to influence others in positive ways. Innovative ideas lead to buy-in and lead to transformation. Sustainable success is quite possible, and from that seemingly innocent exploration years ago, I now have a powerful international organization that is changing lives in positive ways.

Can leadership itself go viral?

For the most part the viral nature of the internet, until recently, was organic. In most cases "going viral" was random, coincidental or just pure luck. Back in 2006, YouTube gave us a platform that was explosive. From crazy cat videos that captivate millions, to revolutionary "as seen on TV" products and instant celebrities being made every day, it was clear that anything and/or anyone can go viral. But that was over 12 years ago.

More typical of today's market, viral content is deliberate and contrived. Media companies, political organization and marketing teams around the world have all devoted serious resources and research into answering the question: "What makes something go viral?" Although good luck still abounds, in many cases, the viral content you are seeing today is a painstakingly contrived result of a marketing scheme. In my own self-promotion I no longer rely on luck to market my services and sell my courses. I engage in deliberate approaches both online and offline to create viral success.

At this point, with all the buzz about viral marketing, viral videos, viral learning etc., I wondered about leadership. Can leadership go viral? In the academics of leadership, we study transactional leadership vs. transformational leadership, various leadership models, and various ways to develop leadership. Since earning my doctorate in Transformational Leadership from Bakke Graduate University on 2013, I have spent the last 5 years studying and defining what "Viral Leadership" is as well as develop a systematic learning platform to refine, advance and teach duplicable Viral Leadership traits.

Think for a moment, what kind of transformation could you make in your organization as a Viral Leader? The possibilities are unlimited through Viral Leadership. As on the internet, in mainstream pop culture or even an actual medical outbreak, going viral can emerge anywhere and at any level. Viral Leadership has the potential to transform everyone and can reach far beyond the initial organization. It can influence an entire community, a town, a country and even the world.

As a professor teaching Transformational Leadership to graduate students I have seen countless new students enthusiastic and eager to learn the traits of great leadership. Until recently, learning about leadership was predicated on what is known as reductionist thinking.

Reductionist thinking comes from the Cartesian method mindset. This is the predominant approach to solving corporate problems, managing people and trying to understand leadership. It identifies what the desired outcome is, brainstorms a tool to fix it, and applies the solution. In a company, the problem might be declining sales, or a lack of innovative next generation products, or trying to predict the future needs of the consumer. Often, new talent is introduced in the form of a new manager, executive or board members. Countless team meetings identifying the problem and then smaller meetings incrementally implementing a solution then follow. Sometimes this new talent skips the meetings, and just dictates the methods that he/she found effective somewhere else and waits for improvement. If it works they stay, if it fails they move on.

Viral Leadership operates at a different level. It does not look outside to fix what is happening inside but instead releases those who are stakeholders at every level to create solutions, innovation and new models. Real progress happens when people are focused on solutions and desired outcome, rather than on obstacles. While a reductionist model seeks to solve a problem, a Positive Psychology approach allows everyone to embrace solutions and because of this, outcomes then exceed any expectation.

Using a Viral Leadership approach also makes Appreciative Inquiry an effective tool for corporate leadership. If you are not familiar with Appreciative Inquiry, we will address it later in this book. In a nutshell, it is an approach to discovery that looks at what or organization is doing well, even during periods of difficulty, defines the strengths and creates a collaborative story that can guide a business. When I uploaded my first YouTube video I expected maybe a few hits and was amazed at 1000 hits. Then the unbelievable happened until a previously unknown therapist in rural Kansas was seen by millions of people all over the world, and the result ultimately transformed psychotherapy worldwide.

Movie Star Innovates Makeup and Creates a Brand

Lights, camera...ACTION!!!! The glitz and glamour of Hollywood have invoked an exciting vision for many throughout the years, as they fantasize their name in bright lights and walking the red carpet. This very dream came true for screen and stage legend, Catherine Hickland. Catherine has enjoyed a long and diverse career on both the screen and the Broadway stage, and is best known for her award-winning role as Lindsay Rappaport on the soap opera, *One Life to Live*.

In this line of work, special attention to hair and makeup are an essential part of the job. Remember Billy Crystal's character, Fernando, proclaiming, "It is better to look good, than to feel good?" Well, that adage really holds true in this case. Stage and screen performers must wear heavy amounts of makeup. It is not uncommon for them to have to spend hours every day in the makeup chair BEFORE they can start working their craft. After years of sitting in the makeup chair, Catherine wound up developing her own techniques and as a result, would be camera ready within a quarter of the normal time. Others soon noticed and began asking for her secret. Being her own makeup artist, she soon realized the frustration of getting exactly what she needed from one supplier. This in turn led to the birth of "Cat Cosmetics." She went to work developing her team, which included a makeup-chemist to custom blend the perfect potions. The result is a systematized collection of everything needed in one, comprehensive makeup kit for women over 40 who have unique makeup needs.

What began as a solution for her own needs evolved as she shared her products with others, making her investment in Cat Cosmetics without real direction, no specific plan but just an excellent product. Then something happened that can only be described as an unplanned viral moment.

During an appearance on the Rosie O'Donnell show, Rosie turned to Catherine and said, "So I heard you started a makeup company?" That moment was the breakout for Cat Cosmetics. Catherine told us, when we interviewed her for this book, that within two days of that simple mention on the Rosie O'Donnell show, $60,000 worth of orders were placed.

Viral Leadership is about taking a moment and creating lasting transformation. Plenty of businesses have unplanned exposure on TV and then can't fill orders, can't re-target customers, and fail to build something lasting from the moment. But, Hickland is a natural born leader. She was a leader in both daytime and evening television, and in other successful entertainment avenues. And she knew that this moment was a make or break moment for her. She quickly identified what she calls her "triangle of success":

- Acquire the customers
- Provide an outstanding product
- Give even better customer service.

Using these simple principles, which really encapsulate the foundation of authenticity and intention that are the foundation for the Four Quadrants of Viral Leadership, Hickland parlayed this moment of viral recognition to an 18-year success story as the CEO of Cat Cosmetics. (On a side note, Revlon didn't get a female CEO until 2018, which I think is bizarre for a cosmetics company!). She has built a team of employees and partners who share her vision of creating unique products specifically for women over 40. Her innovation has created a product line that is as good for the everyday use as well as for professional make-up artistry. She has viral ownership not only from her team, but from her customers, by providing incredible follow-up and customer service. Her customers can engage directly with her on social media, email, and at events she hosts to showcase her product line.

The result has been a growing business that has been able to navigate changes in the economy, changes in style, and even changes in how cosmetics are used, tested, and advertised. All four of the quadrants are there, and from that flash of viral exposure on the Rosie Show, she has been able to build a solid brand to offer something unequalled and unique in the cosmetics business.

The outcome? Happy customers, happy employees, and for Catherine, something with sustainable success has lasted almost 2 decades, surpassing fickle television ratings and network changes.

Innovation Changes Communities

OnMobile is a pioneer in mobile entertainment and sound for mobile phone carriers across the globe. As a mobile service specialist in emerging and high-growth markets, OnMobile services are used by over 1.5 billion mobile users in 55 countries every month. If it weren't for Kiran Anandampillai and his skills of Viral Leadership, this may not have been the case. He did what the Alchemists couldn't, he turned lead into gold and transformed a company that was failing in the great telecom crash of 2002.

It took ten years to go from a fledgling company with less than $300,000 in assets to a publicly traded company with tens of millions in annual revenue, and now operating on multiple continents. Where others had given up hope, Viral Leadership in product development transformed not only OnMobile, but eventually the communities he served. During this time, an amazing story of leadership emerged as Anandampillai not only saved his company, he also become India's "software engineer of eye care." He did this by disrupting a market providing poor eyecare and created a vast network of quality eyecare centers throughout the country for those least able to afford it. He literally took the skills of software design and applied a foundation of leadership, becoming the software engineer of eyecare to tens of thousands of people in need. This is exactly what innovative ideas do in Viral Leadership.

In this case, the Viral Leadership was intentional leadership from a Viral Leader that created lasting change and, more importantly, industry wide and nationwide adoption of real solutions. The rest of this book will share with you the secrets of developing Viral Leadership and the secrets of harnessing it when it emerges organically.

CHAPTER FIVE

Quadrant Three: Ownership and Buy-In

When businesses talk about buy-in, what exactly do they want bought? Ultimately, it is their final product. But the buy-in is the vision and the vision comes from the leader's intention. When businesses talk about ownership, they are talking sometimes about actual ownership, but on a broader spectrum they are seeking buy-in and ownership of the vision. One must be cautious, though, because a vision that is just a platitude from the corporate mucky-mucks is a vision that will never see the light of day. As we learned earlier, when every stakeholder shares the vision (the viral community) it becomes a part of them and drives engagement in the culture, as well as in the outcomes.

Buy-in, according to business legend Randy Dobbs, means that "leaders no longer have to *drag* the organization into the future. The organization begins to *lead* the change into the future state." Many organizations have attempted to gain buy-in, not through leadership but through 'selling' an idea. This comes about when a company's founder, executive, or management team decides FOR the people what *they* think is the best vision. They introduce the idea to others by trying to convince them that this is a good idea. In most cases, if there is no organic buy-in, these upper management ideas are sent down as executive orders or as new company policy. People, however, prefer to make their own choices and for the most part will resist being told what to like.

For over 20 years, co-author RJ Banks worked in the music business as a radio DJ & music director. "Back in the 80s," he says, "we all had our own markets. As the station's music director, it was my job to stay in touch with our listeners and provide them with the music and content they desired. I kept logs of the station's request lines. I would have pizza listening parties with groups of our core demographics. I had relationships with area club DJs. The local music stores sent me weekly sales reports, so I knew what music people were spending their hard-earned money on. This gave me the information I needed order to stay the #1 station in town."

This approach gave Banks' sales team powerful numbers with which to impress clients. It was a successful (Viral Leadership) team and they had created a win-win situation for everyone. Station listeners were happy with the music THEY wanted to hear, sales staff was happy with the ratings numbers, advertisers were happy with the ad results and the radio station was happy because they were making great profits. This was 100% buy-in, buy-in from a viral community created by Viral Leadership.

Unfortunately, in a classic move of greed and a testament to the adage, "Don't fix what's not broken," the radio industry destroyed itself. By the late '90s corporate takeovers and monopoly law dissolutions hit the radio industry hard. Buy-in from the station's on-air and sales staff, the listeners, the advertisers, the clubs and record stores were all lost forever. RJ says, "In what seemed like an overnight transformation we, like most of the other stations in the country, were quickly bought, sold, consolidated, and taken over by big broadcasting corporations. The next thing I knew, I was being told what to play by some guy named Pat. Pat was a music director, but Pat lived in Dallas Texas. I, however was in Santa Barbara, California. Pat would email me a list every week of which songs to add, which songs to drop, as well as how often to play them. Pat worked on the 26th floor of a big, fancy building in downtown Dallas and his company controlled the music for over 30 stations nationwide! How does Pat know what my market wants, likes or dislikes?" Well, long story short, Pat didn't know and Pat (or anyone else for that matter) could not program a radio station from 2000 miles away!

"I still remember the moment when I knew this "corporate" programming thing wasn't going to work. I received my orders from Pat one day and on the top of the "drop list" (as in stop playing) was a song titled "Straight Up" by a new unknown artist named Paula Abdul. Paula, and her song, "Straight Up," was a smash hit in our market at that moment. My request lines were off the hook! It was the #1 dance song at the clubs in town and it was the #1 selling album at the record stores! Santa Barbara loved Paula Abdul! She came up from LA and made a few appearances at the stores and clubs, even visiting our radio station to take calls from her fans! This was an amazing viral extravaganza – a win-win for everyone.

But, as corporate policy dictates, Paula was dropped from the playlist and I was mandated to only play the songs Pat instructed me to play. These "Pat" songs may have tested well in other markets, but they were not liked or accepted in Santa Barbara. It is very apparent that Pat's programming choice had no effect on Paula's career, however, our station and its parent company went bankrupt within 18 months of the transition." RJ's salient point to this story is that by eliminating the nerve center of the business, the viral community that had been created, the entire company collapsed. You cannot force feed your clients and tell them what they like. People know what they want and will adjust accordingly to receive it. For the listeners, it was as simple as changing the channel to another radio station. The moral of the story here is that you cannot create genuine buy-in with fakery.

Creating Viral Buy-In

I have always been a believer in paying people well. When I first joined the workforce, it seemed no one ever wanted to pay me what I was worth or even what I needed. Although I am filled with gratitude for those early career opportunities, like many other people, I was paid minimum wage. At this bottom level of the working class, my job positions were disposable and took no real skill to perform. Later, in my early professional experiences, I remember negotiating for my salary, which, told me that the employer's goal was to get me as cheaply as possible, perhaps even pitting me against others who would work for less pay. This also showed my ignorance as a new employee.

And while I was able to negotiate a wage I knew was higher than another new hires, I suspected that I probably was not being paid as much as they may have been willing to pay. I understand why this is the standard *modus operandi* of business compensation. There are benefits to this practice, ideally motivating workers to learn more, work harder and aspire to a better place. These were dangling the proverbial carrot in front of my hungry face. But, as history shows us, that doesn't really work and in many cases leads to, "It's not my job" and, "They don't pay me enough to care" attitudes.

Over the years, I have consistently overpaid my employees. I have paid them well when times were good, and maintained their pay when times were rough. I have also always preferred to give a salary, plus commissions. This insured that their basic compensation took care of their needs. The commissions, on the other hand, motivated them by allowing individuals to write their own paycheck with success. Even in non-sales positions I have tied weekly "commissions" to overall company objectives. As you read on, you will find we cover other ways to create viral buy-in that go beyond compensation. Let's face it, acquiring money is largely why people work.

When people see or hear stories about how these big corporate executives receive millions in bonuses and shareholders receive incredible dividends, the other side of the story is not so bright. All too often the shadow side of monetary success is riddled with stories of management beating down the wages of workers to increase profitability for themselves and those whom they answer to. This "success" formula has the classic makings of a toxic corporate culture with a very short future.

As with many other businesses around the globe, major airline companies here in the US have been slowly creating a new normal by giving us less and less and charging us more and more. It wasn't that long ago when I could book a flight and check in with 2 or 3 suitcases at no additional charge. I would enjoy full meal, order as many beverages and peanuts as I desired, and never pay an extra cent!

Today, to increase their profits, these same airlines offer far less pay to their staff and in turn far less customer service to their passengers. These US-based companies undoubtedly offer an extremely inferior product compared to Asian, Middle Eastern and other worldwide airline companies. It is very apparent in the negative headlines these US airlines continually receive. The media is quick to highlight tales of dragging passengers off planes, killing dogs, and how billboards are erected by employees warning airlines that they are discontent and are ready to strike. With the current low fuel prices, cutting legroom, decreasing amenities, along with charging extra fees for luggage, food and beverages, profits are soaring! This viral greed is rampant, as evidenced by the recent gall of Frontier Airlines who, believing passengers have the obligation to pay their flight attendants' salaries, are now hitting customers up for tips!

There is no doubt these airlines are screwed-up. I am typing this right now while traveling on an airplane and I am surrounded by the misery they have created - more specifically, by the lack of viral buy-in displayed in their work and attitude. The customers around me are sardined-in, elite flyer benefits are slashed, and customers must pay a minimum of $25 for seat selection. The icing on the poor service cake is an added fear of being arrested at the command of overstressed flight crews.

There is absolutely no buy-in at any of the US-based air carriers. At this point in time, the airline companies are holding the cards. With the currently cheap fuel prices this model will work for those misguided executives, but only for a short time. They are oblivious to how bad the product they have created really is and when fuel prices climb again, the economy becomes weak and demand slacks off, the tables will turn, leaving them wondering where the customer loyalty went.

Think about our gas stations for a moment. Back in the day, pre-mid-1970s, pulling into a gas station was like pulling into the pits at the Daytona 500. You pulled up and 1, 2, or even 3 guys would run out to greet you with a smile. While they were filling your tank with gas, they would wash your windows, check your wiper blades, check your tire pressure, and check your oil and radiator levels. You received this customer service for about thirty cents per gallon and you didn't even have to step out of your car. Nowadays, you get out of your car, pump your own gas, wash your own windows, and check your own oil. For about three plus dollars per gallon, you do all the work!

So, back to creating buy-in. Simply paying people adequately is not always enough to get buy-in at the deepest levels. It sure does go a long way, though, toward setting the stage for buy-in because it reverses the paradigm. It shows that we, as business owners and managers, believe in our employees rather than making them prove they are worth it. For the past two years I have had an electrical engineer working for me, doing computer work and now he's doing some marketing work as well. And although he plans to get a job directly in his field someday, I pay him well enough that he not only stays for the money, but he is genuinely happy here on my team. Someday he will move on, but for now, he is enjoying the perks no other job is going to give him - perks like lunch with me 5 days a week at top of the line restaurants and giving him access to my car when I go out of town on business. This job is not his career and we both know it. This was originally set up to be a part-time job for after he graduated and while seeking a job in his field. As one of my team players, he has learned so many new skills, and has had so many new experiences. In fact, he has decided to start on his master's degree instead of looking for an electrical engineer job. When he leaves for school we will continue to work together online and I will continue to pay him well.

So, this guy benefits and I do, too. In two years I would normally have contracted with 20 cheap outsources to do the work he has done. I probably could have saved a lot of money but investing in someone helps me feel far better at the end of the day. Eventually he will move on, seeking greater opportunities armed with his formal education and the Viral Leadership lessons he learned from working on my team. I am very proud of his work ethics and grateful for the opportunity I enjoy as one of his role models and mentors.

RJ has a great story about buy-in that hits the nail on the head; it's about showing respect to your team members. In his words:

"I realized early on in business that if you take care of your people, they will take care of your business. I also learned, by observation, that if you don't compensate your employees fairly, they will do it themselves, but with your resources. Examples of this are: Extended breaks. Even an extra 5 minutes per day equates to 25 minutes per week. During a month, that is over an hour and a half (100 minutes) of unproductive pay you are doling out. And that is just for one person! Now imagine having a staff of 50 people, all sneaking in their extra 5 minutes per day. That tallies up to a massive 5000 minutes, or 83.3 hours per month you are paying out for unproductive man-hours. To put it into a monetary perspective, even at a lower end wage rate of $10 per hour, the amount you are paying for your 'They don't pay me enough to care' employees is an absurd $9,996.00 per year. That is only four dollars shy of ten grand!

Another sneaky little tactic along these lines is to clock back in, just in time, and then go back to the breakroom to finish watching the last few minutes of your soap opera. Other common self-compensation schemes, all on your company's bank roll, include such seemingly simple things as checking one's email or Facebook, cell phone texting, talking and listening to voicemails, using the company paper, ink and copy machine. Even more aggressive pilfering tactics start with taking items like pens and paper clips, then staples and then the stapler, batteries, and the list goes on and on, sometimes escalating into big ticket items. Restaurants suffer when employees help themselves to food and beverages or even treat their friends to free product. Remember, this is all at your cost!"

In 1993, RJ was a part owner of a major recording studio in Los Angeles. At that time the going rate for a house second engineer position was $18 per hour. Many interviews that result in a job offer also offer less than desirable compensation. The candidate will often accept the job, and the lower pay. They will say, "Yes..." out loud and then complete the sentence under their breath or in their mind with, "...until I find a place that will pay me what I'm worth." What happened here was the hiring of a temporary worker with no loyalty, no buy-in and with the added risk of losing business and customers because of their unprofessional and uncaring attitude.

While interviewing an applicant for the second engineer position, RJ decided to offer him the position. RJ explains, "I remember telling him everything on his application looks fantastic and I'd like to offer him the position. I then said 'But, unfortunately, I cannot pay you the $18 an hour you are requesting.' At that moment I watched his demeanor go from excitement to (slight) disappointment. But then I said, 'The best I can do is $20 an hour.'

The look on his face was priceless! He was so excited yet confused as well. 'Twenty bucks an hour? I don't get it,' he said. I said, 'Yes, you are worth twenty bucks an hour to me.' I remember him walking out the door that afternoon with his head up, his chest out, an air of pride and confidence in his step. Chris, or C Wood as we call him, went on to become our head engineer and had 100% buy-in. As far as he was concerned, this was HIS recording studio business, and he treated it as such. I never once worried about him stealing, fudging his time card, or any other dishonest or disruptive behaviors."

Co-Creation Creates Buy-in

Buy-in is not a onetime action, it is a continuous and ever-evolving culture. This is what happened at Zappos.com. "Powered by Service" was the slogan under their logo for many years. Zappos' mission statement shouts, "To Live and Deliver WOW!". In the Holocracy® model, buy-in is essential among every employee. When Holocracy® was introduced at Zappos, many people left the company. In fact, nearly 17% of the work force abruptly quit. These were people who didn't share the vision of the radical change in role and structure. The media pointed to this as a huge blunder with their new model. What people rarely note is that over 83% stayed and have been co-creating ever since. The reason Zappos.com adapted such a radical model was because of their commitment to service, and they wanted to empower every employee at every level to serve the customer well. The whole adaption of Holocracy®, in this case, was about co-creation.

Co-creation must start somewhere. With the onset of the next project or the next transformation in your business, you have an opportunity to create buy-in. You can become a Viral Leader and ignite your team by allowing leaders at every level to create a culture of buy-in; even customers can be a part of the buy-in culture. By listening to channels of communication, from social media to customer feedback responses, you can amplify the strengths they are articulating and focus on the positive. What resources can a company dedicate to co-creation? Is it every employee at every level, as in the case of Zappos.com? Can teams that usually don't interact, work together on co-creation? What about offering a contest to inspire that creativity? By opening it to everyone in every department, you give yourself the opportunity to discover and create new and innovative ideas that otherwise might never have been realized.

Deutsche Bank is now challenging anyone to "Share their vision of how Artificial Intelligence can help Deutsche Bank reinvent its customer service experience." They are also offering a $30,000 prize pool to discover new ideas. They are conducting this worldwide search through the website, jovoto.com, a creative workspace that is open to anyone. This is co-creation at its finest. Imagine the difference in marketing between A: "We now use artificial intelligence to control your money" and B: "Through innovative ideas, we have created the future of banking in a digitalized world." The contrast co-creation provides is astonishing. Deutsche Bank isn't the only company using jovoto.com as a co-creation forum. Companies like Coca-Cola, Victorinox, Knorr, and even UNICEF are using "crowd storming" as a way of collaborating and co-creating.

Buy-in by Sharing Vision

When crafting a vision statement, the number one mistake companies make lies not within the statement itself, but in how the vision is, or can be, used to create buy-in and viral enthusiasm. A typical format involves either hiring an outside consulting firm, or a small team of employees are tasked with creating a vision statement. The result is then introduced to everyone via a meeting or presentation. Next, leaders must try to gain buy-in from the rest of the team by attempting to convince them how awesome their vision statement is. At this point, instead of sharing an inspirational vision, the process has become a sales job. Sometimes it's an easy sale and there is immediate buy-in; more often, the obvious objections are overlooked, or the misleading nature of the vision statement is obvious. Other times, there is cognitive-dissonance between the vision statement and the beliefs and visions of the stakeholders.

To share a vision, co-creating a vision is necessary. A few years ago, I wanted to refine my own vision statement, so I started reflecting on why I offered products and services. To gain insight, I sent my team a simple survey, anonymous and online, with one question, "What word would you use to describe what we are doing right?" I then created a word cloud with the results. When I presented the completed vision statement to the rest of the team, I began with the word cloud - letting everyone see the actual words they submitted being used. This was a fun and exciting way to show how their responses were the foundation of the viral vision and the approach we would be using.

The result was lasting buy-in. And, when several years ago, one of my associates suggested I lead with "why" in promoting an upcoming event, I pointed to her help in crafting the vision statement we developed a few years ago and how we were already accomplishing that.

Gaining Buy-In in Other Ways

"Can't buy me love, love... money can't buy me love" is a viral refrain from an old Beatles' song. Although money can contribute to buy-in, the single most important factor in the buy-in of ideas is rapport. In Viral Leadership, rapport is what opens the doorway to successful buy-in of the vision. Without rapport, leadership will probably never go viral. Without rapport, your efforts are just meaningless ideas from clueless managers who don't do any of the real work. And while this perception may be oversimplified, once it takes hold in a corporate culture, there is likely nothing that will overcome it, other than rapport.

Rapport is the communication that creates effective relationships and takes them to a level where there is shared vision. Steve Jobs and Steve Wozniak had a shared vision. Jobs sold his Volkswagen bus and Wozniak sold his calculator to generate the start-up capital needed for their little company called Apple Computers, Inc. They took the risk and felt the enthusiasm to grab the brass ring because they shared a vision. But where did it begin? How did these two connect with this shared vision of the future? It began in 1969, at Hewlett-Packard where Jobs was an intern and Wozniak worked as engineer. It was here that a friendship was started and, in 1976, it was here that the vision was created in the famous garage. Genuine friendship creates rapport, hallmarks of which are mutual attentiveness, positivity and being in sync with one another.

By building rapport with others, we open pathways to opportunities, partnerships, collaborations and most importantly, the unification and development of a vision. Many executives talk about sharing vision, but vision is best shared through the framework of rapport. As a leader, sharing workspace with employees and team members, as well as meals and other activities, creates rapport. Renowned business author and speaker, Zig Ziglar, stresses trust in selling and noted that relationships are everything to a company. He famously said, "You can get everything in life you want if you will just help enough other people get what they want." And what people really want is to be heard, to be valued and to be included as part of the team.

Building rapport begins with an introduction. Meeting new people and simply saying, "Hello, I am Richard" sets a friendly tone and puts the wheels are in motion. In large organizations, where upper management and executives are known only by their pictures on the wall or in the business news, there is no need to assert a title. People already know who you are, but what they don't know is that you are a real person. The most effective and sincere way to meet team members and open rapport involves simplicity, authenticity and even a bit of humility. I have found that my simple introduction and a handshake is often followed by, "Of course. It's so great to meet you." At this point the next few lines will be dictate the depth of the acquaintance and future relationship. This is because decisions about likability are made by the subconscious mind, made almost instantly at a primal level.

Looking into someone's eyes, whom I have just met, my next line is a reciprocating, "I, too, am glad to know you!" and immediately followed by an open-ended question about the other person. For example, "Tell me about your work here?" or "What contribution are you making in this department?" By using this formula, I immediately engage one of Robert Cialdini's principles of influence: *reciprocity*. Reciprocity is activated by affirming that I, too, am happy to meet them, and encourages rapport and partnership.

By asking an open-ended question about them, I communicate two very important things: Firstly, it's not about me, it's about them. Even if I am the one with the official title, this form of humility opens communication and rapport. Secondly, this approach appeals to a known fact that people know about themselves best and generally like to talk about themselves.

This simple formula works in business as well as in every other type of relationship. Do you want more friends? Follow this formula. Do you want romance and love? Follow this formula. Do you want better relationships with your children, neighbors or anyone else? Put these principles to work and you will be opening doors rather than closing them. Whether I am meeting new people or interacting with people I have long term relationships with, my approach is the same - I ask them about themselves.

For rapport to take hold, common interests must be shared. This is where the beginning of viral buy-in takes place and where we find entry points for sharing our vision with the goal of complimenting the information we receive. This must come from a genuine spirit of desiring collaboration. Simple, yet powerful gesticulations, ranging from eye contact to open body posture, facilitate these initial conversations and display one's open and friendly personality. Open doors vs. closed doors in offices, giving out cell numbers rather than screened office numbers, and being available are all common strategies that are rarely taken advantage of or abused by employees.

Advance rapport building comes by remembering details and following up on the cares and concerns of the people we meet. This is important. Remembering names, and remembering their interests communicates a lot when we later ask for buy-in. When RJ Banks was a young music director at a radio station, he would receive calls from innumerable record companies attempting to influence him to pay their music on his station. To most, he was just another name and number on the weekly call list. But one of these reps was different.

"Every week when Joe called me he would ask me about...me. He always remembered things about me and my family, my mom's name, and even her birthday! He'd say stuff like 'Didn't you say a while back that your mom's birthday is in March? Well our artist Celine Dion is going to be performing there on her birthday! Why don't I send you a couple tickets to the show and then to a late dinner with her after?' While most people are amazed at the awesome gift package being offered, I'm thinking "Wow! This guy remembers MY mom's birthday!" That, my friends, is rapport. I later learned that all he does is keep a simple spreadsheet with all the little bits of information he learns about me. How? By simply asking questions, and then documenting the answers. Whenever he called me, I was up on his screen. My cat's name, my mom's birthday, my girlfriend's favorite flower, where I went to college, and the list goes on! Whatever information he would learn about me and my life, he would document it. So simple, yet so effective."

Maintaining an info sheet on people in your circle is such a simple, yet effective way to stay informed and connected. When RJ was a department head, he had a staff of sixty-two. That's sixty-two names, their birthdays, and more than triple that amount of details when including their spouses and children's names, likes, dislikes, etc.

By using questions as the approach of appreciative inquiry, we are literally co-creating a story with those we lead. I love questions like, "What is the best way we can conceptualize the future?" or, "What is most important to you in this project?" or, "Why is this personally interesting or important to you?" These are all great questions to ask that result in shared co-creation. A book I used in my doctoral work was titled, *Appreciative Team Building: Positive Questions to Bring Out the Best of Your Team*. It is a book I recommend to everyone interested in deep rapport skills.

There are also techniques of non-verbal communication that can make a huge influence on rapport building. I do a lot of keynote speaking and training sessions. Almost every public speaker will tell you that openness is an important non-verbal communication strategy. You never see a professional speaker touch a podium. Almost every professional speaker, if given a podium, will stand back a bit or to the side, avoiding the temptation to lean on it, shake it or hide behind it. Managers and executives hide behind memos, hide behind doors, and hide behind blame-shifting – coming out from hiding helps create genuine and dynamic rapport.

We also recognize that many of our communication strategies are evolutionary and when we become stressed, anxious or not confident, our natural tendency is to "cover our vital organs." In communication this is indicated by folding arms across the chest or putting hands into pockets and covering the sides. And, just like in a fight between two animals on the Discovery Channel, this communicates that we are unsure or vulnerable. To exude confidence, be open and keep the hands free, the palms visible, and be relaxed. This is a much more inviting way to communicate and says that we are here to create partnerships rather than to discipline, judge or cajole others into toting the party line.

Once rapport is created and trust is established, sharing visions and mission statements, along with corporate values, becomes easy. It becomes easy because this process invites feedback and contribution, which is more effective than a top-down visions statement that is sold and force-fed via a meeting or a memo. People, which include employees and customers, are resistant to change; by encouraging them to be a part of the change, we gain buy-in.

Appreciative Inquiry (AI) has long been my favored process in creating not only transformation, but buy-in. AI is a process that discovers and exposes the strengths, talents and potential in leaders and employees alike. This includes customers, community and stakeholders all coming together to explore resources. AI is essentially rapport-building through an organization. It has been used by companies large and small, from General Electric to John Deere. Hospitals, community-based social services, and companies in merger and acquisition have used it to bring cultures together and create a new vision. According to CBS news, to solve the problem of declining sales, customer dissatisfaction and failed cost-reduction efforts, John Deere launched ten new strategic business opportunities. The result was improved esprit de corps and a savings of $3 million in product-development costs.

AI can be conceptualized as a series of interviews to discover what is working. AI does not focus on deficits and problems because the goal of AI is long-term transformation that draws on strengths - the highlight of using AI is that it is an entirely positive approach! The ultimate tool for building rapport companywide, it merges stories and shows relationships connecting departments, divisions and leadership. Companies often hold an AI summit to begin the process and celebrate the conclusion by sharing results in a subsequent summit. This creates a feeling of inclusion and values everyone's contribution.

During periods of change, such as merging cultures, changing markets or policy changes, getting buy-in makes a huge difference in success or failure.

CHAPTER SIX

Quadrant Four: Culture of Engagement

Company culture drives Viral Leadership. It is the culture of an organization that determines its success or failure. Creating a culture of engagement is essential in creating a lasting transformation. Chances are pretty good that you work at, or have worked for, a company that has a toxic culture. The good news is that culture can be changed. Mulally at Ford went right after the toxic culture and brought the company back together. It was a culture of engagement that saved Ford from the failures GM and Chrysler simultaneously experiencing. (Mr. Mulally is no longer with Ford; currently, Mary Barra at GM holds the highest star in the automotive industry). Company culture is the outcome of the accumulative beliefs and behaviors of the individuals that make up a company. A company's culture emerges over time via traits, personalities, habits and patterns. Although MBA courses and books attempt to define culture in various ways, company culture is something that goes beyond definition – it is felt. It is felt by employees at a visceral level, and by management and customers.

To exemplify my point, here are my personal experiences with Starbucks and a different national chain serving coffee and breakfast. Let me start by saying that between the two, I am a long time Starbucks patron, but am always open to choices. On my way to the office early one morning, I noticed the competitor in my neighborhood. As I approached the entrance, I remembered wanting to try their new smoked sausage breakfast sandwich. I was so hungry and so excited to indulge in this culinary masterpiece as depicted in the image plastered on the window that was as big as my car. Upon entering, I immediately noticed that the store was in disarray and the employees seemed a little chaotic. While making my order with the seemingly less than enthusiastic woman behind the counter, I was abruptly informed that their equipment had a problem and they could not make a sandwich. I nodded and left, noticing how she failed to apologize for the inconvenience, not even offering me a doughnut or other consolation prize. But, I thought that was okay; there is another one of these stores next to my office.

As I drove toward my office and the other shop, my mouth was watering, and my stomach growled in anticipation of that delicious, smoked sausage sandwich. It was no longer a craving; it was now a mission. Arriving at competitor #2, but still not impressed by the surroundings, I placed my order. I then waited. And then I waited some more. After what seemed like way too long, the disinterested clerk held a bag up and simply said, "Here!" I grabbed the bag, took it to a table, and opened the bag...only to find out it was the wrong sandwich. It was a flat breakfast sausage on a croissant. I returned to the counter and politely informed the clerk that she made the wrong sandwich. She responded by abruptly saying, "Oh, no. We are out of the other. But that's still sausage." I admit I was a bit taken back by her snappy attitude and lack of customer service. Because I was now late for an appointment and I was hungry, I thanked her and left, dutifully eating the sandwich I was given.

About a week later, I was still craving that new smoked sausage sandwich offered by the competition of Starbucks. I again stopped in, and although I received the correct sandwich this time, I started to observe the store more closely. Its culture had really set in now, and I began to compare it with my experiences at Starbucks. This store was minimalist - the furniture was inexpensive-looking, the dining room was a mess. The clerk who helped me was unfriendly and appeared irritated when my colleague changed his mind about which doughnut he wanted. I once again placed a smoked sausage sandwich order and once again, I waited, and I waited, and waited. Finally, I heard a loud and irritated, "Here!" again. Since I was the only person waiting, I knew it was mine, so I walked to the counter. I never even saw the employee who served it. She was already gone, off doing something else. No smile, no thank-you, just a bag on the counter. As I walked out of the store I compared it in my mind to my experiences at Starbucks, where they always smile and know my name.

A now-famous quote from Starbuck founder and former CEO Howard Schultz is, "*...at Starbucks, I've always said we're not in the coffee business serving people, we're in the people business servicing coffee.*" The Starbucks culture values employees at every level – including providing well-paying jobs with health insurance benefits even for part-timers. The Starbucks mission statement reads, "*Our mission: to inspire* *and nurture the human spirit – one person, one cup and one neighborhood at a time."* They do not give numbers to customers or simply yell, "Here!"; they ask you your name, write it on your cup and call you by name when your order is ready. The organizational structure is diverse, inclusive and promotes bonds among employees. The company is extremely philanthropic and helps individual employees as well as entire communities and their members.

Certainly, no company will ever be without any challenging issues, complaints or disgruntled employees, but Starbucks has excelled in retaining employees and making people feel valued. When I googled the competitor's store name and "corporate culture" I found a very unique website called comparably.com. This website collects, evaluates, and posts company ratings based off of employee questionnaires. The competition earned a D+. Feedback on comparably.com consistently rates this company in the lowest percentiles in areas ranging from diversity to environment to meetings. The website gave a CEO score of "bottom 30%". When I left the store that morning, I again had a visceral response of disappointment. It also appears the employees have the same response.

Next, googling "Starbucks Company Culture" led to front page results where journalists praised and extolled the example of Starbucks. Eric Flamholz, a managerial consultant that was part of Starbucks initial launch, pointed out that the "secret" to their success is not magic beans, but the strategic vision, leadership and management – the people of Starbucks. They have created a culture of engagement and propelled it to viral success. This culture of engagement is known not only by its customers, but also by the employees.

The "not my job" or the ever so famous "they don't pay me enough to care" mindset is an outcome of company culture. Starbucks has a distinct company culture and I have experienced it in every Starbucks I have been to from the Starbucks in my local community to Starbucks I have visited in Singapore, Beijing and Europe. Starbucks, by the way, displays an A+ at comparabably.com, and the new CEO Kevin Johnson is rated in the top 5%. I am not familiar with the real objectivity of this website, but what they reported mirrors my experiences.

Mulally proved, with his transformation of Ford, that cultures can be changed. In other words, there is hope for the Starbucks competition to improve, and it is quite possible that Starbucks could lose the lead. This is one of the greatest thing about culture, it can be changed. Stratospheric changes have occurred in American culture, and the same is true in business. The paramount question is not, "What are the problems in a culture?" but, "How can leaders create a culture of engagement?" I am stressing the word engagement because this is the key characteristic of building a culture in the context of Viral Leadership. Engagement creates involvement. It invites response, and it recognizes that at every level, culture can be created, activated and perfected with ever-evolving developments and enhancements.

GE's Randy Dobbs wrote, *"When you want to create a new culture, you are inspiring people to modify their core beliefs – who they are in business."* Leaders who wish to enhance the cultural experience should note that a company is comprised of people, and people are only limited by their beliefs. While coaching and counseling leaders in my practice, I have found that it is self-limiting beliefs that stand in the way of activating change. Examples are beliefs like, "The company isn't ready for change," or, "We have to replace some key board members before we can even think about change." While some people who hold limiting beliefs can stand in the way of progress, by transforming ourselves first, we can create a subconscious desire by others, even stalwarts, to embrace new possibilities. This can only be accomplished by maintaining congruency between intentions and vision. The intention to share, with a strategic vision based on why we do what we do, can transform a business culture. It is infectious and won't be hidden under a bushel. Congruence between intention and vision is something that manifests as positive action, becoming noticed so that others want to be a part of it. This is the definition of Viral Leadership.

In the 1980s, as our culture moved into the tech-age, a more open and desirable cultural climate of engagement within these types of companies began to evolve. We've all heard the stories about the CEO playing ping-pong with the mailroom clerk in the middle of the day, while at work. Although this laissez-faire culture has had its critics over the years, there are several companies in business today that are great examples of offering a successfully engaged cultural climate.

Businesses such as the website building company: Squarespace, as well as the Adobe Systems Company are examples of this. Year after year, Squarespace has been voted one of New York City's best places to work. The Adobe Company is on this same level and adheres to the same philosophies and cultural beliefs. These two entities have successfully created a culture that thrives by reducing layers of management between front-line employees and executives.

It's not Holocracy® but is a "thin" organizational chart that values the entire company working together in an "open" model. This makes everyone accessible to one another most anytime and at every level, which results in transformation in a genuine way. These companies show that they value their employees by providing top pay, huge perks and great benefits. But most importantly, they have created an engaged culture through Viral Leadership and showing respect to their employees.

What is it that most often stifles communication and decision making? More times than not, the answer is: layers and layers of bureaucracy. This is something that flattening can easily solve. At Squarespace.com for example, the employees are truly heard. Likewise, the Adobe Company created a culture of engagement by unleashing the creativity of their employees. They achieved this by bringing lifestyle and quality of life to the corporate culture. They even have a hashtag for it: #AdobeLife. This was created to foster a sense of improving the quality of living for their employees. At Adobe the annual employee performance ratings are not used to "grade" their employees' performances. They choose to stay away from micromanaging, finding that this methodology promotes a sense of freedom in doing one's job, which results in enhanced levels of creativity. Employees are empowered to contribute and more importantly they want to – because they feel as if they are part of the vision – and they are, and this again is the definition of Viral Leadership.

What is it that these companies are doing that you can do? How can you work hard and play hard as a team? Adobe does it by presenting challenging projects and then empowering employees to find solutions without being babysat. Can your company provide greater autonomy to unleash creativity? I say the answer is a big, Yes. By paying attention to the work-life balance, you will engage your employees in the real world. What is it that you do, or can do, to demonstrate that you care about your employees at every level?

I remember one of my first jobs in the restaurant business, it was at Chi-Chi's Mexican restaurant. The first month I was there, it was rough. The place was always packed and everyone, including management, yelled at each other. Speaking of the managers, all three of them would hide in the office and only emerge when the restaurant got busy. When they did emerge, it was usually to yell at us for being "in the weeds" and to pressure us to go faster and turn tables quicker. I arrived at work one day to find out that the General Manager had been replaced. There were two corporate big-wigs there and they introduced us to our new GM, whose name was Chuck.

Chuck's first duty was to appoint a new assistant kitchen manager. The person he chose for the position worked as previously the dishwasher! Chuck spent the next couple days in the kitchen working as a line cook. He left us (the waiters alone) and it just felt like that old stress had melted away. Over the next couple months, I never heard Chuck yell. If he saw a problem, he grabbed a tray and cleaned a table. He helped employees lift heavy trays and boxes, and he expedited food to the tables. He was a great boss because he respected and inspired us by leading through example. He told me he started in fast food and moved to a full-service restaurant as a line cook. He worked his way up, and he led his team by helping them make things run smoothly. He didn't say much, but he engaged everyone in both the front of the house and the back of the house.

The company, H-E-B (you pronounce the letters), operates 350 grocery stores throughout Texas and northern Mexico. The letters H-E-B stand for Howard E. Butt. Although the name sounds like a schoolyard insult, it is the actual name of the company's founder. Nowadays, the initials also stand for "Here Everything's Better," the store's slogan. Hyperbole? Maybe...maybe not. I remember shopping at H-E-B because they had the best tortillas I had ever eaten. H-E-B believes every person counts and it is one of the few grocery store chains I have been to where the managers are easy to find. At H-E-B the bar is set high. According to the Harvard Business Review, Craig Boyan, H-E-B's President and COO, calls the culture "one of *restless dissatisfaction* striving specifically to engage more, serve more and innovate more." And this desire for engagement is reflected in how employees are titled. As a matter of fact, they are not called employees, but rather, "partners."

Boyan's principles of performance and engagement translates to the community as well. This is one of the key aspects of Viral Leadership, which does not just lead or motivate employees, but garners engagement from all stakeholders, including both customers and the broader community. In 2015, Boyan was honored by Texas A&M University with the McLane Leadership in Business Award. The award specifically relates to the fusion of business and service and, with Boyan at the helm, H-E-B has been at the forefront of community service. This includes everything from disaster relief to food bank assistance to an open call for non-profits to partner with H-E-B for direct support. These facts about H-E-B can be found by reading about the company. Even though I have not lived in San Antonio for many years, I still love my trips there. Why? Because not only do they still have the best tortillas in the world, but because every time I have walked into their store in the 25 years, it has been a positive experience. A culture that engages is culture that is visible.

These examples can encourage you to create an incredible corporate culture. The takeaway here is that if you hold limiting beliefs about your team, about the community, or about engagement, you will be limited by those beliefs. But, by being open to new possibilities and engaging your team at all levels, you can adapt new beliefs, which will result in new actions.

Mulally at Ford demonstrated that even a global company with toxic culture can change direction and do so rapidly. Barra at GM show us how to infuse innovation and forward thinking into the company culture. Starbucks competition models how not to treat customers. Boyan at H-E-B shows us that by partnering with employees and the community, we - the company - become valued. And what becomes valued, becomes valuable. Adobe proves us that by moving away from micromanaging and allowing for creativity, we will enhance engagement and enhance outcomes. Squarespace shows us that leadership can be engaged at every level, even if everyone is not a "boss". And finally, people like Chuck, the GM at Chi-Chi's where I worked when I was in college, show us that engagement comes best with leading by example.

PART THREE

Foundations of Viral Leadership

CHAPTER SEVEN

Foundation of Intention

The foundation of harnessing the power of Now and creating lasting transformation is intention. Nothing that exists in this world exists without intention. A desk does not make itself, a car does not build itself, and even an autonomous vehicle had to be programmed by someone with intention. Intention is what creates our reality and it is for this reason that it is the foundation of leadership.

After dropping out of high school because of his struggles with English, Richard Montanez began his thirty-five-year career with the Frito-Lay factory as a janitor.

Much like Ford's inspirational CEO Alan Mulally, and Virgin CEO Richard Branson, the Frito-Lay Company practices the same philosophy of everyone being a part of the team. One day a message from the company president was sent to all Frito-Lay employees encouraging them all to "act as owners of the company", no matter what their position. This inspired Montanez to do something big. He set the intention of expanding the Cheetos brand to include a spicy hot version inspired by Mexican street food. This is really a beautiful story illustrating the power of leadership to inspire intention. That message from the president set employees at every level free to believe and encouraged to dream...and dream big! Montanez was so excited and inspired that he called the president's office and scheduled a meeting to pitch his product idea.

He and his wife had been developing recipes and flavor combinations, having set the intention of sharing their heritage and tastes with the world. Two weeks after making his call to the president, Richard Montanez bought his first tie so that he would look professional at his meeting. Today, Flamin' Hot Cheetos are Frito-Lay's top-selling product! Richard Montanez is now known as the "Godfather of Hispanic Branding" and after 35 years with the company, he retired from spearheading the Hispanic marketing team in his role as a Senior Executive.

Montanez teaches us a valuable lesson: it is our intention that often sends an idea or a product into the viral orbit. The Flamin' Hot Cheetos didn't just taste good. They become the Number One selling Frito-Lay product and have helped lead Frito-Lay to a 56% market share in the salty snack category. Montanez followed the leader (the company president) and become a leader himself. Over his 35 years with the company, he also brought new flavors and new profits to other PepsiCo companies like KFC and Taco Bell. His Viral Leadership also spread from the company to the community. This included giving the community scholarships, school supplies and a desire to open doors for Hispanic youth.

People can often forget the importance of intention. In our career training we had intention to finish a degree, complete a certification program or master a craft or skill. As we worked towards our chosen goal, our intention was being fulfilled and it brought rewards along the way - rewards such as financial gain, opportunities for advancement, or the ability to assume positions of high regard. But, as we manifested those original intentions, in some cases we became too enamored by the rewards and stopped aspiring to new intention. Unfortunately, even people in positions of leadership can lose focus on intention and get caught up in chasing the proverbial pot of gold at the end of the rainbow.

Marriages can often demonstrate examples of lost intentions. I am a licensed marriage and family therapist with a master's degree in counseling. In 30 years of doing therapy with clients, I have seen the following trend over and over:

A young couple sets the intention to live happily ever after. Typically, the joyful lovebirds will start off working together to reach their mutual goals, hand in hand, with smiles on their faces. First is the intention to get married. The engagement, the parties, the planning, the guest list, the reception, the food, the music, who sits next to whom, and then the honeymoon...details, details, details!

Next comes a new way of life that includes buying a house and perhaps a car. Soon after arrives the family, then getting through pregnancies and childbirth, stinky diapers, sleepless nights, then school, clothes, cell phones, teenagers, and the list goes on!

Eventually, a few years after reaching their initial goals, the previously blissful couple have lost sight of their intention and are bogged down by the life they have created for themselves. They forget that they intended to spend time together, dream together, and grow old together, and they drift apart. The goals are still there, but the intention is not. This is the source of the 7-year itch for most couples.

Unfortunately, psychotherapy is a lot like business and rather than focusing on intention to fix it, most therapists just help people set new goals on top of old goals, making the problems ultimately worse.

One very important distinction I want to now firmly plant into your mind is that goal setting is not the same thing as setting intention. Goals are future-focused, while intentions are present-focused. Intention is what we live and manifest. Goals are what we strive for. This difference is why intention is the foundation of sustaining leadership and capturing the enthusiasm of a viral moment. Intention is a key in noticing the trend and capturing the moment so that we can strategically enhance our leadership.

Have you ever created a vision board? I created one a couple years ago with four pictures. The pictures were the goals I held at that time. One of these was a weight loss goal represented by a picture of me when I was at my best a few years previous. The next picture was the Las Vegas skyline. As my kids were nearing college age, my goal was to move to Las Vegas after they became independent. The next image was a stack of "Paid in Full" bills, representing my specific financial goal. The fourth image was of a beautiful, black, shiny new Mercedes-Benz Maybach. Although I never did get the Maybach, I did get a black Mercedes E550. To date, I am now at a comfortable weight, I love living in Las Vegas, my bills are always paid and, for anyone reading who does have a E550 Mercedes model, you know it's more than enough car, and close enough to count as reaching the goal!

My vision board may have appeared shallow to some as there was no world peace, or lofty goal of unifying cultural divides that have caused great division in our world, blah,

blah, blah. But that is not what a vision board is for. A vision board is to stimulate one's mind, focus on specific desires and activate the actions necessary to reach one's goals. As the Law of Attraction always dictates, I stayed focused and within 15 months of hanging those four pictures over my monitor, my vision board was the first thing I packed in my Mercedes for my move to Las Vegas.

Although goal setting is a very important cog in the wheel of success, it is limited and will only take one so far. Setting goals alone are often not enough to keep one motivated. Intentions, on the other hand, have no limits and open our field of vision, expanding our imagination and visualizing new opportunities. In my case, I had the same four goals for 15 months. And although I eventually hit every one of them, there were times of seemingly little to no progress, especially dealing with the weight loss goals that were gruelingly frustrating and almost impossible.

But, thankfully, every day is a new day to set new intentions. In many ways, intentions are more gratifying than goals, because intentions can be manifested and be immediately gratifying every day. You do not have to wait to be kind, or to listen to others, or to be accountable but can experience these things now with intention.

Research shows us that successful leaders in corporate settings have certain characteristics. Some of these include self-awareness, self-control and resilience. Either goals or intentions can be set around each one of these. I can set the goal to increase self-awareness by practicing monitoring my emotions and I can even use technology to help me measure the outcome. Tools like the Muse, a brain-sensing headband, can tell me if I am spending enough time each day in the mental frame of self-awareness. I can set goals for self-control, like not eating dessert after each lunch and each dinner, or only having soda once a week. I can set a goal for resilience by measuring the time I spend doing things outside of work along with setting a goal to increase these meaningful activities.

But, unlike intentions, each of these goals will take time to be reached. Intention provides instant gratification. In each of these three areas I can set an intention and begin living it right now. For self-awareness, I can set the intention to be aware of my body and sensations in any situation. For self-control, I can set the intention to be good to myself and for resilience, I can set the intention to just breath when faced with stress. And the good news is, I can start living these intentions and reaping the rewards right now.

Alan Mulally led Ford by setting the intention of refocusing on its core brand. The goal was to divest Jaguar and Volvo, but the intention he set was for Ford to be the very best it could be. If you recall, he began setting his intentions on Day One. His intention was to open dialogue and to become a "no judgement zone". His intention was to create 100% employee buy-in at all levels. His intention was to be confident, even in the face of overwhelming financial problems. His intention was not to just return Ford to profitability but to sustaining profitability. The financial numbers were the goal, but the intention was sustainable profitability, and every action, every day, reinforced that vision.

Setting intention is, to some extent, setting into action that to which we are most receptive - kindness, compassion, well-being, and balance. Some intentions are physical, the intention to know and use our bodies. Some intentions can be emotional, to be happy, to be grateful, or to create calm. And of course, intentions can be spiritual, to experience meaningful engagement throughout the day or joy at work.

Intention really is our internal wealth. As leaders in the business setting we are financially rewarded for effective leadership and, after a lifetime of leadership, wealth can be measured by bank statements, cars, and paid-off mortgages. I never believed the line, "Money doesn't buy happiness." I have always found that the more money I have, the easier it is to be happy and enjoy life for myself as well as the pleasure of sharing it with others. In other words, as an entrepreneur I have experienced boom and bust more than once. I find it easier to be happy when I am experiencing boom rather than bust. But, ultimately, I have also found contentment during periods of bust, and the reason I did was because of my intention - my intention to be grateful, and my intention to be optimistic and my intention to see how my experiences could benefit others.

After graduating high school, my daughter took a couple of years off to work full-time and to pursue her athletic dream. She had become a nationally ranked roller-derby contender, a lead jammer, and wanted to travel the country playing her sport. A few years later, around the same time my youngest son entered college at 18, she, too, was ready to go to college. Now, I was prepared for one kid in college, but two at the same time caught me a little off guard. My son decided to get a combined bachelor's/master's degree and my daughter was a Speech Language Pathology major and went full-time on the 5-year plan.

Although my son was a top scholar and ended up getting scholarships to fund nearly 100% of his education in the last two years, my daughter, having entered college a bit late, did not have those same opportunities. I paid for their cars, phones, insurance, and expenses, including tuition, room and board so they would be able to graduate without student loans. And for part of this time, I was also paying for my school, as well as finishing my doctorate at Bakke Graduate University.

As a student myself at that time, I was far less attentive to my business, and earning far less than I had in previous years. But we all made it through school without any student loans. My intention was to live each day debt-free and to stay within the means afforded to me. It was my intention to be grateful for my Ford Escape, even though my goal was a Mercedes- Benz. It was my intention that gave me wealth during the bust years, and it was my intention that created true wealth, happiness, and contentment each day.

What is your intention? Right now, think of what would be most valuable to you in this moment. Chances are pretty good it's not actually a Mercedes Maybach that would be most valuable to you at this very moment. After all, you are not driving your car right now, you are reading a book. You are probably at your desk or at home in a chair. Right now, the intention to learn, the intention to be focused, and the intention to be receptive to new perspectives is far more important than any goal you may also be holding.

Intention harnesses the power of Now. Goals are focused on the future. Intention is where our plans come from and where our purpose and design for living is established. To make sure you never miss a viral opportunity to exercise leadership, set your intention each morning. Self-affirmations are a great way to do this. For me, the most effective method of self-affirmation is to simply keep a dry erase marker in the bathroom and every morning, write my intentions of the bathroom mirror. A dry erase marker and a bathroom mirror are essential tools for any leader. Right now, on my bathroom mirror is this intention: "I intend to share my experiences that can help others through my writing today."

If you don't have a dry erase marker at home, set the goal to stop at the store on your way home from work today and buy some. Then set your intention to inspire yourself by writing your intentions rather than your goals on the bathroom mirror each day.

And as an additional bonus, setting one's intentions also helps in our goal setting. Goal setting is important because, if we aim for nothing, we hit nothing. But intention is often where our goals come from, and more importantly, good intention helps us create clearer and more beneficial goals.

CHAPTER EIGHT

Viral Leadership is Built on Authenticity

Viral Leadership becomes effective when the ideas and enthusiasm from a person gains buy-in from others. As team members come onboard and increase the synergistic energy, the next level of buy-in takes place. There are, of course, many factors at play here, which range from the initial enthusiasm from a core group to gaining full team cooperation. The effects may be for a specific issue or for a blanket policy adjustment. FOMO, the fear of missing out, is also a factor in many cases. It really does not matter what the motivation is at this point as critical mass is established. Historically this pattern is found in almost every viral success story.

Tulip Mania is considered by many as the first recorded viral frenzy. Tulip Mania was a period in the Dutch Golden Age of the early 1600s. During this time, market prices for the popular flower bulbs skyrocketed and then profoundly collapsed in 1637. The term "Tulip Mania" has become a metaphorical term describing any large economic bubble that reaches critical mass and then collapses. But the pattern does not always result in a crash; enthusiasm and buy-in can be sustained. The difference between fads that crash and lasting movements can be defined and differentiated by leadership.

Coca-Cola has a rich history of seizing the moment to create lasting change. When introduced at soda fountains throughout the Atlanta area, Coca-Cola was undoubtedly a smash hit. Investor and majority owner, Asa Candler, saw the frenzy and grabbed the opportunity to expand beyond Atlanta, introducing the concept of bottling to preserve the product for reaching broader territories. Management also recognized the value of branding early on to create lasting enthusiasm. In 1916, the licensed bottlers created a unified message in the distinctive bottle that could be easily identified as unique from their competitors'.

In its one hundred and thirty-year history, Coca-Cola has adapted to world markets, weathered global wars and recessions, and remains today a stalwart company listed on the Dow Jones Industrial Average. Aside from creating a great product with a long history of good corporate decisions, the brand has been authentic. Authenticity is the core that binds product and customer together. Authenticity is the glue that bonds the core of synergy and buy-in. Authenticity, above all else, separates brand leaders from other brands and propels individual leaders to recognition as a creator and contributor rather than "just the boss."

Early Coca-Cola ads seem to reflect the mystical properties promised by its pharmacist creator, Dr. John Pemberton. This magical elixir was advertised and promoted as an "ideal brain tonic" and a way to "impart energy and vigor". It was even promoted as a cure for medical conditions. Coca-Cola had certainly created a lasting formula and enjoyed success at this level for many years. In 1905, a real change in marketing came about with an ad extolling Coca-Cola as a product for all classes. Coca-Cola not only recognized the value of branding, but the importance of continuity companywide. This inspired creating a Quality Assurance system to ensure high standards are maintained, from recipe adherence to specifying the optimum temperature for enjoyable consumption of the beverage. Each of these elements contributes to authenticity by making a reliable product. No matter where in the world you may be, you will more than likely find Coca-Cola on the shelf, in the cooler, or on the menu, and it will taste just as good and refreshing as the last one you enjoyed.

One interesting aspect about Coca-Cola's authenticity early on was a strong desire not to compete on price. From its inception in 1886 and for the next 70+ years, no matter where you went, the price for a Coke was the same. Stability, predictability, and consistency: These are not only the hallmarks of a sustaining movement, but also of leadership and, more specifically, authenticity.

Coca-Cola is a shining example of the effectiveness of WHY *marketing,* as articulated by Simon Sinek in his book, *Start with Why.* Sinek gives us a biological reason for why inspired leaders and inspired companies start with WHY as the power source of success. In his book, he shares example after example of successful companies and leaders who focused on WHY they offered a product or service, rather than the WHAT or HOW. "Products with a clear sense of WHY give people a way to say to the outside world who they are and what they believe." He writes, "Remember, people don't buy WHAT you do, they buy WHY you do it." He then goes on to indict the leadership of many companies who fail to understand leading with the power of WHY, adding, "And when that happens, manipulations that rely on pushing price, features, service or quality become the primary currency of differentiation."

During this same period, Pepsi competed on price and offered twice the ounces for the same price. Pepsi's 1939 slogan was, "Twice as much for a nickel." 40 years later, they were still spending their time, efforts and monies focusing on duking it out with the competition, rather than telling us WHY we should all drink Pepsi. "Taste that beats the others cold - Pepsi pours it on" was their slogan, starting in 1967. The 1970s brought us the Pepsi challenge, still competing to win new customers on taste. Coca-Cola, on the other hand, adapted the slogan, "Look Up, America" and, "Coke adds life." These slogans are reasons WHY rather than WHAT or HOW. Here are just a handful of the many effective slogans that persist being associated with Coca-Cola decades later:

- 1937 – America's favorite moment.
- 1939 – Whoever you are, whatever you do, think of good ice-cold Coca-Cola.
- 1945 – Coke means Coca-Cola.
- 1947 – Coke knows no season.
- 1969 – It's the real thing.
- 1979 – Have a Coke and a smile.
- 1999 – Enjoy.
- 2005 – Make It Real.
- 2009 – Open Happiness.

Each of these slogans, and the many I did not have space for in this book, exude authenticity. They speak to the WHY of Coke. The result has been more than one hundred years of market dominance. This is the value of authenticity. Authenticity is the glue that makes Viral Leadership stick.

At the time of this writing, Coca-Cola is once again in the news. And once again, this positive publicity is directly related to authenticity. More specifically, their number two selling product, Diet Coke, is in the spotlight. For years now, soda sales have been on the decline and Diet Coke has perhaps suffered the most. However, the report I am reading currently is sharing the results of the most recent quarterly profits from Coca-Cola, proving the pundits wrong. Soon after redesigning the old, short, fat diet-coke cans to the more modern and slender, taller cans, sales began to climb. Analysts and other speculators are attributing the success to everything from cloning the look of the popular energy drink, Red Bull, to the new colorful cans appealing to younger millennials who have not yet embraced Diet Coke like their parents.

I suppose it will take a while for the marketing research executive to issue a determining factor, but I can probably save them a lot of money. The new marketing is decidedly authentic. Not only is Diet Coke finally out of its short, fat can (something that always struck me as odd, as someone with behavioral psychology training) but it has been marketed specifically with authenticity as a value. Raphael Acevedo, the executive responsible for the new roll out, even used the word authenticity in an interview with CNN. He said, "We're making the brand more relatable and more authentic." The interesting note here is that this was not a corporate decision hatched in a meeting room, but one that came after two years of efforts and gaining the buy-in of over 10,000 consumers before launching the change. Although one quarter is not enough to define a trend, the long history of Coke being authentic clearly points to continued dominance and maybe even sustainable growth with a product many had written off as dead to the new healthy times.

Viral Leadership is about creating sustenance from an enthusiastic emergence of ideas, products and innovation, something that captures the dreams of people with a common cause. Authenticity goes a long way to capture that enthusiasm and the power of Now. But if companies can be authentic how does this authenticity arise? Aren't company just mindless organizations the make and deliver products? Of course not. After all, businesses are not thought of as people...but, they are. They come into being with the convergence of people and almost every business succeeds or fails based on its people, including leadership. This is true for businesses of every size – even a giant corporation Enron collapsed because of its people.

In Tulsa, Oklahoma, there has been a small mom and pop restaurant called Steak Stuffers USA. Founder George Van Wyck opened it with his wife in the late 1980s. The sandwiches were cooked by their son Garth and his wife. Although George has passed away, the company is still family owned and operated. To this day, they continue to succeed in the tough restaurant business and, get this – in the worst locations possible for a business to try and survive. Garth and his mother still run the store and, contrary to conventional wisdom and business logic, they're only open 5 days a week. (Even Chick-fil-A is open 6 days a week.) Their first location was too small. Their second location of 20+ years had limited roadway access. You had to really want to go there to get there and many previous businesses had failed in that same spot.

Steak Stuffers USA, however, made it work! Not only have they created and offer a great product, they continue to focus on how important people are to their business. They treat their employees correctly with respect, dignity, generous pay and benefits and they treat customers like family, even displaying photos of their customers on an interior wall. Up until his death, George manned the cash register every day and called every customer by their name.

On the other end of the spectrum, let me tell you about Amy's Bakery. Amy's Bakery was a small Scottsdale based restaurant that famously crashed and burned on social media by literally fighting with their customers! They unfortunately met their demise after an episode of Kitchen Nightmares starring Chef Gordon Ramsey. I used to frequent this restaurant whenever I was in Scottsdale. Their desserts were amazingly delicious – perhaps the best I have ever had. Dinner was actually pretty good too. Unfortunately, it was their inability to communicate with people, both staff, customers and social media that decimated their business

The saying goes, "A company is only as strong as their people." We can extrapolate from this statement that companies are only as authentic as their people. If you want to seize the power of Now to create dynamic and powerful success in business – then authenticity is going to be the key to unlock that success.

The internet is littered with inauthentic attempts to make something interesting, useful, or entertaining. These types of YouTube videos get no hits and their FaceBook posts get no likes or shares. In the end, most of these attempts just become a future embarrassment for the creator.

But videos that are authentic, interesting, useful or in some other way capture an authentic moment or people, can easily become viral. The first video of cochlear implant users hearing their loved one's voice for the first time is a great example. Videos of heartfelt proposals that captured the moment rather than a staged production; babies, animals, baby animals...these all get millions of hits. Memes that capture a snapshot of reality become famous, such as people like Kyle Craven, who accidentally became "Bad Luck Brian," or Sammy Griner, who became "Success Kid", while looking tough and holding a fistful of sand when he was just a baby.

How to Cultivate Authenticity

Authenticity is one of those elusive creatures we seem to identify best by first recognizing the lack of authenticity. We have all had that boss who we knew really did not care. We have all experienced the customer service rep who was not interested in service or the salesperson who just creeped us out. True authenticity is understated and we most often recognize it in retrospect. I'm sure we can all think of people in our lives who is or was truly authentic.

What vibe do you give off? Do people receive you as authentic? The good news for us is that psychology researchers have studied authenticity in detail. Alex Wood, a positive psychology researcher, tells us that these three behaviors comprise true authenticity:

Self-alienation - How well we feel we know ourselves and understand our qualities, characteristics and behaviors.

Authentic living - How congruent are our actions with our beliefs and values.

Accepting external influence - How much we adapt to our perception of how others would like us to be.

These are the three focal points for developing authenticity. I am going to go straight to what we can do to perform our best in each of these areas. By developing them, you are more likely to encourage others to share your dream, your vision and act to seize the power of Now:

Self-Knowledge - I am surprised how many executives I coach really lack a clear picture of themselves. They know what they can do, they know they did do, they know what they want to do. But they do not know who they are. They fight with their deficits, often fear their demons, and are filled with self-doubt about their own ability to sustain their position. Most people won't admit their deficits to others, especially a spouse or co-worker, but they know what they are.

I find that what is missing from our frame of reference concerning the authentic self is usually the internal strengths we possess. Sure, we can identify the obvious traits: well educated, hard worker, etc., but what are the deepest strengths we possess? These are the beliefs and behaviors that resonate with our qualities of character: trustworthy, honest, loyal, brave, clean, reverent (sound familiar, Scouts?). Taking a personal inventory is not just to look at self-deprecating faults, but to also identify our strengths. Clearly, PBS childhood television personality Mr. Rogers was viewed by most as authentic. But he was also strong, persuasive, and unwavering - all captured in a timeless video of him which has gone viral in our current era of social media. It is an amazing video of him defending public financing for PBS in front of Congress in 1969.

To learn more about yourself, tangible personality tests such as Myers & Briggs, are widely available online. For me, they are both informative and entertaining.

Create your personal motto - Companies often develop mottos to create and guide their esprit de corps. Start by identifying your values, those beliefs you hold about yourself, your company, your employees and the community of customers. Google has a slogan: "Don't be evil." Adidas has adapted: "Impossible is Nothing", (which is actually an adaptation from a Muhammad Ali quote), and probably the most recognized slogan of our modern time: "Just Do IT", from the fine marketing folks at Nike.

So, what is your motto? Create one. Write it on your bathroom mirror. This will help you evaluate if the choices you are making, the actions you are taking and the associations you are holding are congruent with your motto.

In his book, *Ignite the Secret: 19 Lessons for Business and Life*, CEO Charles Horton, the founder of SecureVital, writes: "Determine your principles upfront, and envision the mission you have for yourself and your team. When you have established your values in advance, you will know when you're violating them because it will start to feel uncomfortable." He continues, "Choose what you stand for, create your own platform, and implement your beliefs into your business."

Flock with inspirational people - Earlier in this book we talked about intention. To develop authentic leadership, you must not only identify your intention, you must then surround yourself with people who both inspire you and that you inspire. The relationship between intention and inspiration is rarely seen. It is when we seek relationships and mentoring from those who are inspirational that our authentic intentions rise to the top. Horton gives sage advice when he says, "Figure out who has something to teach you and pursue that person's company and advice." To be authentic we need to be both mentors and mentored. It is critical you choose your mentors wisely and chose those who are positive, grounded and inspirational.

CHAPTER NINE

Go V.I.R.A.L.

A leader's job is to lead - and the place to begin leading is within oneself. Qualities and attributes of effective leadership are musts for all leaders, especially Viral Leaders. Without focusing internally on our own strengths and personal development, it is impossible to coach and lead others. When leaders develop their potential and enhance their own internal resources, behaviors and personality characteristics, the very process of doing so becomes valuable. I have found that it is a lot easier for me to help people make positive change when I have made those changes myself. This gives me empathy for difficulty, it gives me the ability to share with others from a place of passion and experience, and it helps me to enthusiastically engage with others.

So far, I have shared countless cases and examples of Viral Leadership along with the specific pathway to harnessing the power of Now to create lasting transformation. Now it is time to focus inward. Here are the big five factors in creating viral success with your leadership:

Vison
Integrity
Role Model
Action
Loyalty

Each of these have been explored either directly or indirectly in previous chapters. And each of these five factors can be utilized and developed differently in each of the Four Quadrants of Viral Leadership.

Vision

Vision is about taking today's intention and stepping into something lasting. Vision is often mistaken for a roadmap to the future – but we really have no idea what the external factors in any given business will be in the future. Effective vision involves extending intention into something lasting that is not rigid. Flexibility, and being "lightweight", allows an organization to move into the future unencumbered by a fixed map. You can think of vision as being much like a flight plan for a cross-country trip. Although the pilot files a flight plan with all the markers along the way, once in the air, the pilot will deviate from that flight plan based on present conditions, weather, speed, winds, air traffic, weight and many other factors, as necessary. It is intention coupled with experience and insight that guides the flight, not the filed flight plan.

Vision is practiced and developed – it is much like intuition to some extent. In this context, vision is a character trait rather than the often discussed "Vision Statement." Vision, as a character trait, exemplifies clarity of thought, requiring an ability to use discernment to clarify what is important and separate it from what is unimportant. It is the ability to take something small and conceptualize it in a larger context.

In the First Quadrant of Viral Leadership (Creating Viral Teams), vision is unveiling the potential in everyone and contains the ability to conceptualize how various players can share the vision. It manifests in the Second Quadrant of Viral Leadership (Innovative Ideas) by seeing beyond the obvious. Steven Sasson, a young engineer at Eastman-Kodak and the inventor of the digital camera, did exactly this. He put various components together, including a lens from a super-8 camera, a charge coupled device, a cassette recorder, batteries, and electrical circuits to create a machine that allowed an image to be stored on tape and then played back later. No paper, no film, and completely self-contained. It was the attribute of vision (perhaps from his engineering background) and his ability to transcend the obvious and be innovative that disrupted a market.

It is worth noting that 33% of Standard and Poor's CEOs hold engineering degrees. Engineering is a discipline that specifically focuses on training skills in vision and innovation. In the Third Quadrant of Viral Leadership (Ownership and Buy-in) vision again emerges as Viral Leaders seize the power of Now. Vision is action, and action comes from vision. Having vision of how to act upon the Now is an ongoing process that will maintain enthusiasm and growth throughout the organization. In the Fourth Quadrant (Culture of Engagement) vision is again manifested, as a shared vision is created from the experiences and values of every stakeholder.

Interestingly, despite Mr. Sasson inventing the camera as an engineer working for Eastman-Kodak, the company did not share his vision. Eastman-Kodak even went so far as to allegedly suppress his invention, not bringing it to market because they feared it would cannibalize their lucrative film income. Leadership at Eastman-Kodak, like with so many other companies, was focused on maintaining the status-quo and not on innovation. Kodak has become case study number one in numerous articles and books about the importance of vision in disruptive innovation. Forbes characterized it this way, "There are few corporate blunders as staggering as Kodak's missed opportunities in digital photography, a technology that it invented. This strategic failure was the direct cause of Kodak's decades-long decline as digital photography destroyed its film-based business model." And I will characterize it as a failure to create a corporate culture that cultivated vision.

Integrity

Integrity offers the opportunity to share intention and vision in a way that is genuine, and to gain full-hearted buy-in as the result. Integrity and authenticity go hand in hand. When it comes to building teams, First Quadrant success is created from trust. One of the universal needs of all people is security and, like authenticity, which is felt at a visceral level, integrity is also one of those needs.

Integrity is also innovative. In the current world political climate, most everything seems rather surreal. Relationships and friendships are increasingly virtual. Even things that are established fact, such as the planet earth being round, are up for grabs anymore. The result of what is really a time of truth-angst, is that the trifecta of genuineness, authenticity and integrity instantly stands out from the crowd. I have a colleague that makes marketing videos and posts them to his vlog. After a few weeks of being absent, he returned by sharing a personal tragedy in his family. But rather than seeking sympathy, he had clearly made his latest video out of the spirit of authenticity. He stated he was at an emotional loss of how to proceed and genuinely asking for help. He even acknowledged his embarrassment over sharing personal details, but felt he had no choice. This is a powerful form of integrity - a leader recognizing his own need for leadership (in this case personal and emotional) and owning his limitations.

Integrity innovates by being unique - it really does stand out. It is one way to solve the problem many start-ups face in recruiting talent that cannot yet be afforded. Optimistically though, history is filled with experienced and talented people joining new or even fledgling businesses. They come onboard because they believe in the integrity of the leaders and of the project. History is also filled with stories of incredible rewards for individuals and the companies they have aligned themselves with. This innovation leads to buy-in and ownership as well as a culture of engagement.

Role Model

Viral Leaders are role models. They manifest leadership both at work and in the community. This is one of the great things about leadership; effective leaders don't just lead in one position or in one area of life, they transfer that leadership to every area of life. For example, practicing various forms of meditation has gained in popularity over the past few years.

And now with meditation timer apps, people are competing for the most meditation minutes, much like a pseudo-spiritual FitBit. People are reporting they are now meditating 20 or 30 minutes a day. Others are besting them with reports of 40 or 60-minute sessions. But the value of meditation is not in how many minutes one meditates, rather the goal of any meditation practice is to be able to extend the value and process to everyday life. In other words, 2 minutes or 20 minutes of meditation really does not matter. What does matter is: does one become meditative? Likewise, leadership is not about role or level, it is about being able to make the world a better place. True leaders lead, not only at every level, but in every situation.

This automatically results in team building. Everyone loves the significance of being part of something greater than themselves, and you are innovative in this role, transforming the lives of others. Being a role model extends across all four quadrants of Viral Leadership, creating ownership and buy-in and creating the culture of excellence. It is easy to change a culture when an organization is filled with role models.

Being a role model takes vision and integrity. Being a role model helps others learn to lead by example. The best way to train others in leadership is to let them see leadership in every situation. Practice emotional intelligence not only at work, but also in your families, with your children, and with strangers in the coffee shop. The result will be a transformation across every part of your life.

Action

Viral Leaders take action. Successful leadership is intentionally created with deliberate ideas. The Doubletree cookie from our first chapter is one example, but it was the action taken that ensured success and valued branding that is the hallmark of leadership. Viral Leadership can also come from organic or even accidental successes. But again, the calling card of Viral Leadership is seizing the moment - and that comes from taking action.

Action can, of course, be taken across all four quadrants of Viral Leadership. Creating Viral Teams by communicating with all members, it opens the doorway to involvement by all stakeholders. Action is essential in launching innovation. I often wonder how many great ideas have been thought of but never materialized because no action was taken. Innovation cannot be separated from action.

Action is required for ownership and buy-in. The action of building teams culminates in viral success when there is buy-in. Buy-in and ownership requires work, ongoing communication and feedback. It needs to be processed like Appreciative Inquiry to reach critical mass. But, once buy-in is achieved, the rewards are limitless for almost any company!

The number one hindrance to success for almost every business is a lack of engagement. Action that increases engagement leads to lasting transformation in business. Actions that can be taken to improve productivity include:

Treat your team with respect.

Provide them with the tools and environment the need for peak performance and productivity.

Let them be heard and pay them enough so they are invested in success – and reward success with bonuses at every level.

Train managers to be more effective and give them insight into solving issues of productivity. This will increase the sense of buy-in as well as create a culture of engagement.

The general manager who can pick up a table during a tough dinner rush, or a kitchen manager who can jump onto the line, can increase productivity by showing employees that they are with the employee rather than simply "bossing" employees. Strategies that create a culture of engagement are actions that encourage and support employees and set an example. We have all seen the "Do as I say, not as I do" manager. Actions that "Do as I do" are far more effective at creating long term success.

Loyalty

I prefer to hire people who demonstrate loyalty, even if they lack skills. Why? Because skills can be taught but loyalty cannot. Loyalty, as a hallmark of Viral Leadership, is not just about employees, but about the attributes of leaders as well. Are you loyal to the vision? Loyal to the employees? Loyal to providing the customer experience that they believe they are purchasing?

Viral Leaders are loyal to the teams they create, not just to the success of a team. They help a team come together and stay together in tough times. Viral Leaders train and build up others. Even though each member of the team has an individual position, the Viral Leader encourages them to function as "one for all." Viral Leaders manifest loyalty in innovation by staying true to their own intentions. They also set new intentions to help the team rise to an even higher level. This is a great thing about Viral Leadership, it never stops! It continually builds upon previous successes and becomes self-replicating.

Viral Leaders create and manifest loyalty through buy-in and ownership, treating projects and people as having the worth that comes from a shared experience. Viral Leaders create cultures of engagement through loyalty. A company culture with loyalty can not only transform an establishment, it can sustain it through some very challenging times.

PART FOUR

Specific Ways to Activate Viral Leadership

CHAPTER TEN

How Intention Leads Us into Action

Intention leads us to action by opening our hearts and minds to the possibilities around us. Intention is the foundation of Viral Leadership because it helps us to direct our actions in ways that allow us to seize the moment. Have you ever missed the moment?

When I was 14, the movie, The Black Stallion, came out. There were 7 kids in my family and going to the Libertyville Theater was a big deal. Now, I am sure my folks told me what time to return when I took off to ride my bicycle in the neighborhood but, being a typical young boy, I lost track of time and, of course, back in those days we didn't have cellphones. I still remember being mortified when I saw our green "Woodie" 1973 Vista Cruiser station wagon pass me on our street. My step-father was driving, my mother was talking to him and my sisters were playing in the back. Nobody saw me. I yelled and yelled, but my screams clearly could not be heard by anyone in the car. I rode my bicycle as fast as I could to catch them at the stop sign, but my peddling was no match for the Oldsmobile V-8, even in a tank like our wagon.

As they turned onto the main road, I knew I would not catch them, but that did not stop me from peddling as fast as I could, in hope that I would be noticed in the rear-view mirror. I cried. I cried hard. I remember riding my bike home to an empty house and going to my room and just crying in my pillow. To this day, I still haven't seen that movie. And to this day, I have an inner drive and intention not to miss out on the things that are important.

If the foundation of Viral Leadership is intention, then the framework is action. Nothing else can get done until some sort of action is taken. In leadership training we often look at action as a strategy. A good example of this concept is taking the action to build trust or action to communicate clearly. Relating to Viral Leadership, there are three main types of actions. These actions complete the framework and allow the viral moment to become a sustaining movement.

They are:
- Action to launch viral energy.
- Action to engage more people in the experience.
- Action to move forward from the moment and into something sustaining.

1. Action to launch viral energy

With the intention to provide unique and high-quality board games, the company CMON Ltd. has successfully used Kickstarter (a crowd-funding website) to fund and successfully launch over 27 board games. This clever and unique company specializes in hand-painted "mini" characters for their games, which sets them apart from others. In 2016, they were one of the top 5 highest Kickstarter customers to generate and receive funding for their board game, *Massive Darkness*. With the viral success of that game, which retails for $120.00, they flourished and became a publicly traded company. To date they have raised over $38 million dollars in Kickstarter funds for various projects. This amount of financial support is incredible for any board game manufacturer, especially one specializing in hand-painted "mini" characters.

To create a sustainable business model from the viral launches, CMON Ltd. widened their market footprint by acquiring other websites and companies that support the board game industry. Because they took action to fill a specialized niche, they have even found success in creating and publishing a periodical gaming magazine in an era of declining print publications. Fostering continued enthusiasm for their products and their industry as a whole, they have organized game painting competitions with professional level prizes and cash purses for overall winner.

The action of CMON Ltd. and CEO Mr. Ng Chern Ann has not only been focused on creating viral marketing within the Kickstarter platform, but to create sustaining leadership through its other actions. Unlike other game makers who have achieved Kickstarter success, actions to sustain the viral success and launches with retail partners have created a worldwide base that would not be possible with just a website.

How exactly does something become viral? The hula-hoop, the Ford Taurus, and the DoubleTree cookie all preceded the internet, yet they share the same characteristics as the post-internet successes. Think of those miniature board games raising $38 million dollars, or Justin Bieber as a legacy in the music industry with a Number One YouTube channel and Twitter account with billions (yes, billions) of hits and tens of millions of followers.

In the mid-1990s, as Hotmail was introduced as a free email service, the employees of Hotmail were amazed at how many new member signups came simply from "word-of-mouth" through internet blog forums. WIRED magazine editor, Bill Wasik, reports that it was these employees who coined the term "going viral." From that time on, "going viral" has been a major objective of every teenager with a camera, business with an underfunded new idea, and every entertainer - both professional and amateur. In fact, I cannot think of a single industry where gaining viral attention would not be of benefit. I can also guarantee that executives in most every boardroom in the world spend time, at one level or another, trying to discover and develop their company's viral niche.

In analyzing what becomes viral, it is apparent this can happen without any seemingly logical rhyme or reason. Whether the viral surge was intended or unintended, through the internet or not, certain characteristics seem to be present across the board:

- Something Noteworthy
- Something Entertaining
- Something Astonishing
- Something Useful

You can create interest and viral energy and begin a movement by tapping into these common characteristics that others have had. Look for ways to inspire, unite, and amaze. Look for ways to give something of value to people and look for ways to entertain people to increase the likelihood of supercharging your potential audience.

You may be surprised when the results of your actions exceed your wildest expectations. The Ford Taurus became a bestselling car because it was useful, it had noteworthy style changes and model improvements over the years. The DoubleTree cookie is useful. What sets them apart from any other cookie is that they are also astonishing. Store bought cookies are notoriously dry or fake gooey, but the DoubleTree cookie is simply amazing. Although the actual recipe is a secret, internet recipe cloners almost always have a combination of milk chocolate, oatmeal, cinnamon, vanilla extract and brown sugar. The result is a cookie that will even impress your grandmother.

Justin Bieber is a multiplatinum recording artist because he is entertaining and astonishing. If you are a 14-year old girl, you might say he is also useful and noteworthy. There are a lot of Justin Bieber haters as well, but his videos went viral and his career was launched. Unlike one-hit wonders or musical trends that have long since disappeared, his music, acting and social media career has had staying power. Bieber is an entertainer, and a master at it. Unlike other childhood stars, he has transitioned into adulthood as a leader in the music industry. Yes, he did throw eggs at a neighbor's house, but he is also very involved in charities that build schools for children in underprivileged areas. By being involved, I mean at a Jimmy Carter level. He has been a part of the on-sight construction crews hammering and nailing the wood. Sure, some bad press covering his teenage love triangles and stupid stunts made the headlines but even these things garnered him more notoriety and more hits.

In the end, even if you don't like his musical style, he is a phenomenal entertainer and, dare I say, leader. Millions of people are Beliebers and his music is loved by millions. He also took action on his viral discovery and had the business sense to listen to Usher and his other adult coaches. He continues to interact with his fans on a personal level and even encourages them to sneak into sold out concerts!

Another of my favorite "viral" stories from the internet is of comedian and inspirational speaker, Judson Laipply. In 2006, he created the most watched video on the internet called, *Evolution of Dance*. To date he has received hundreds of millions of views and still growing. He was smart and parlayed his viral video success to his profession. Laipply's would never have achieved such success as a headlining comedy act and keynote speaker without his crazy dance video in an Orange Crush t-shirt.

Speaking of viral videos, one of the earliest I remember becoming enthralled with was called, *Did You Know; Shift Happens - Globalization; Information Age*. About the same time this video came out I was deep into my career and profession. I had written a book about cross-generational culture tapping into changing markets. I was a frequent keynote speaker at conferences around the country addressing this topic. In this viral video, facts and figures were presented that both astounded people and provided information. Much like TED talks that have become viral, the information presented was highly actionable and the music it was set to helped create an almost hypnotic entry point into a new digital future.

I remember early days in the infancy of the World Wide Web. This new thing called "email" quickly became the quickest and most popular route of textual communication. One could send and receive written correspondence around the world within seconds. It was amazing! Not only could one communicate textually, but one could also send and receive documents and even photographs. Email gives us the ability to share content with the click of a forward button. Many of the earliest viral messages on the internet came in the form of email. Today on social media, Pinterest, Instagram and tweeting have become the most popular platforms to share food pictures, makeup artistry, and amazing images of beautiful things. In each of the preceding examples, you can see these elements at work in the viral success of either planned or unplanned events.

2. Action to engage more people in the experience

The action that is most likely to create viral growth is an action that engages the first follower as a co-leader. Action that engages is action that builds a movement. Something fascinating happens when one person takes the lead, and as others join in, critical mass is created. FOMO (Fear of Missing Out) is a powerful tool in creating viral awareness and people want to be the first to share, the first to participate and the first to "go all-in." Understand this, and you have one of the keys to creating and building from viral experiences.

I had a boss for a few weeks once that had to be, in the history of bosses, one of the worst bosses ever. The company I was working for had been sold by the founder to a larger corporation upon his retirement, and that is when I was hired. The new CEO was a compassionate woman who had clinical experience as a physician, but little administration experience. She was appointed by the new company but was hand-picked by the founder. She did her best and knew her limitations, and so she convinced the larger corporation to hire another new CEO and move her role to one managing only the clinical aspects of the business. It really was a mess, and the organization was in turmoil at every level.

The new CEO was named Mark. He was young and fresh out of MBA school. I am not sure how much actual experience he had, but he came in the first day, held a staff meeting and let us know he was breaking the culture that was unprofitable and that he was the "bus driver" now. He literally held a staff meeting with a stick figure drive he labeled as "Mark" and then added the rest of us in the back of the bus as stick figures he was driving. He put us in order from front to back as to how important he saw our position in relation to one thing – profitability. He told us he was driving the bus and that the bus was not stopping! He then told us to jump off the bus if we didn't want to go along for the ride, illustrating stick figures bailing from the bus and hitting the sidewalk.

That is not the way to inspire action. The action I took was to get off the bus. It was only a matter of weeks before I jumped off the bus, and I have never looked back on that decision.

3. Action to move forward from "the moment" into something sustaining

To create something sustaining, you must create community. CMON Ltd. did that by creating social contests for gamers to meet in real life, and monthly magazines to connect people in their niche. In my primary business I have done this by creating pages that celebrate an idea rather than a page that celebrates me or my business. The business comes naturally from providing something of value to a community.

I am very active on social media. From millions of hits on my YouTube channels to hosting large professional groups on Facebook, I have learned how to make the social media platform both beneficial and profitable. Unfortunately, my observation is that most people interact in the wrong way. I see real estate agents who create a business page promoting, "Anywhere Real Estate", and other business owner posing pages asking people to "like" their pizza place, Botox office, shoe store, or consulting business. They have obviously tended to these pages with great care and even have spent money on these pages either through advertising or buying graphics or paying an assistant to curate items for it.

Despite these efforts, it is very seldom they receive the desired results. The cause is simple, there is no reason to "like" the page of a real estate agent, unless of course it is your sister, husband or best friend. And even if you amass a lot of "likes" through paid advertising, nobody is really following the page anyway. Most professionals promoting their business fail to create something sustaining from their efforts.

As a licensed psychotherapist, I have trained thousands of other professionals in both the clinical and business aspects of building a practice. There is really no reason for anyone to "like" a mental health professional's page. Pizza shops get a little bit of organic action, but those people are probably existing customers fishing for a coupon. A successful social media page can accomplish a lot:

- Customer retention
- Attract new customers
- Build loyalty

- Share product applications and instructions
- Increase sales

But none of these can be accomplished by just creating another meaningless advertisement page on the internet. When I train medical professionals, I advise them not to create a business page, but rather a community page. Social media is about engagement, it is about community. What is most important to consumers of social media is friendship and connection, not product and services.

I advise them to create a social media group about their city or region. Rather than the Dr. Joe Schmoe's private practice page, create a community page. Something like a *DallasisAwesome.com*! This marketing tactic works for any business and in any city. On your community page post topical and relevant information and keep it current. Remember the 4 elements of a successful viral campaign:

- Something Noteworthy
- Something Entertaining
- Something Astonishing
- Something Useful

Update the weather, share local business news, post memes and tidbits of viral content that relate to your city. The sport teams, or the people, and celebrate your city! When I did this as part of a training seminar a few years back, we ended up getting over one million pageviews in less than three days. People joined and liked the page in droves.

Co-author and editor of this book, RJ Banks, created a topical community on Facebook and currently has over half a million members in his group. One may ask, what is the value of having these followers? The answer: engagement, or, action to move forward from the "moment" into something sustaining. Banks' "moment" came when he first posted his downloadable *Morning Affirmations* sign. RJ has been selling his book, *The Power of I Am and the Law of Attraction,* as well as his audio affirmations programs to his community members for years now. When you create a community page you control that page and the engagement; stop by every week and let people know you are a part of that community and where they can buy a house, get a pizza or buy your book. You can share the services you offer whether they are medical services, consulting services, or accounting through an ongoing portal for promoting within the culture of social media that will really work for you.

CHAPTER ELEVEN

Leadership for Everyone

Viral Leadership is not dependent on a CEO, manager, or anyone with a specific title or position. Viral Leadership can emerge naturally at any place and from anyone within an organization. We all have a business, be it local or part of a national chain, which we frequent because of that one employee - that one employee who make a difference and makes us feel special.

In 2014, I was having dinner with a small group of friends at a local Las Vegas restaurant. One is a physician friend, another works at the front desk of a major hotel/casino in Las Vegas, and one manages a large health and gym studio. As we were all talking and visiting, I was telling them about my project and this upcoming book on leadership. When the conversation turned toward the life-changing impact one person can have on another person, Linda, the hotel front desk clerk, told us a story. This wasn't a story about leadership per se, but it is one that I see as a perfect example of effective leadership.

A few years back, Linda was excited about the upcoming holiday season and her first Christmas working at the hotel. With the holiday season upon them and the delight of

Christmas joy everywhere, Linda realized that some of her teammates would be alone for the holidays. She knew that somebody on her team would not even get as much as a card. She knew that somebody on her team of 84 people would feel lonely, unloved and alone. She thought about it and then took action. What she did next was inspiring and revealed her true compassion and natural leadership qualities. What she did next was not a corporate directive or "orders from above." What she did next was done with kindness and consideration.

During her time off, Linda enthusiastically designed and hand-created 84 individual and unique Christmas cards. She created and personalized a card for every member on her team. She then snuck into work before her shift one morning and secretly slipped the cards into each of their mailboxes, wishing all on her team a Merry Christmas. Now, keep in mind she is not the team leader; she is not a department manager; she is not the president of the company. She is a front-line employee like the other 84 employees on her team. What she did through kindheartedness and thoughtful consideration is as powerful as any decision the CEO can make. This type of leadership becomes involved in the community and these natural leaders become the ambassadors for the brand. They create enthusiasm among other employees and energize the entire team. My friend has no desire to move up the ladder. She is very happy and content and will probably work to her retirement in her same customer service position. But her leadership has created tradition, esprit de corps, and positive impact in the workplace. She has been doing this for 3 years now and the tradition has spread to other departments and even other businesses. My friend, Linda, is a true viral leader.

With the encouragement and mentoring of such great high-level executives as legendary GE Chairman Jack Welch, Randy Dobbs rose to become one of the company's top CEOs. Throughout his career, he developed a strong reputation as a turn-around specialist. He has transformed every department and organization he has led. His formula and natural leadership have increased earnings at every level.

In his book titled, *Transformational Leadership: A Blueprint for Real Organizational Change,* he gives us five attributes that define Transformational Leadership.[1] These are all based on what we can see in the results.

These are the 5 key elements of Transformational Leadership according to Dobbs:

- Build a culture
- Improve *esprit de corps*
- Communicate issues and actions
- Change the financial, behavioral/spiritual or other metric results
- Leave behind a cadre of future transformational leaders

Remember, anyone at any level can be a part of all five of these elements. In fact, in viral contexts, it is likely that leadership will emerge at any level. Remember the story of the Flamin' Hot Cheetos? He was the janitor. Effective leaders recognize that leadership can emerge at any level and effective leaders *encourage* leadership at every level. By

---

[1] Randy Dobbs, *Transformational Leadership: A Blueprint for Real Organizational Change*, 1st ed. (L, Ar: Parkhurst Brothers Inc., Publishers, 2010).

reserving "leadership" to those only with titles and positions of authority, creativity is stifled. The culture and work environment become toxic and people feel as if their efforts don't count. Echoing back to Sir Richard Branson's quote, "Take care of your people, and they will take care of your business", it is the feeling of worthlessness from management that drives your people to seek other opportunities elsewhere. Remember, "buy-in" at all levels is imperative for Viral Leadership.

In their bestselling book, *Transformational Leadership*, authors Bernard Bass and Ronald Riggio write: *"Leadership is not just the province of people at the top. Leadership could occur at all levels and by any individual."* Traditionally, the process has been leaders training potential leaders below them, thus retaining the metaphor of a hierarchy. I see vertical structuring of leadership as a poor metaphor. For example, Linda, who makes the Christmas cards every year for her fellow team members, is not trying to get to the top. She is, however, connecting to people in a meaningful way. This action, in turn, connects those people to each other in a meaningful way regardless of where they are in the company's pecking order.

Stanford professor Bob Sutton argues that hierarchy is not a bad thing. In his book, *Scaling Up Excellence,* he writes that it's both inevitable and needed.[2] Sutton, however, is speaking in the context of organizational management, and while I agree that hierarchy as an organizational concept that is both inevitable and needed, leadership transcends

---

[2] Robert Sutton, "Hierarchy Is Good. Hierarchy Is Essential. And Less Isn't Always Better" http://blogs.parc.com/blog/2014/02/hierarchy-is-good-hierarchy-is-essential-and-less-isnt-always-better/ (accessed March 8, 2014).

hierarchy. It really is much more personal, which is why everybody can be a transformational leader. Even within the hierarchy or organizational structure, leadership can be present or conceptualized as a matrix with hierarchical, lateral, and even bottom-up incarnations.

Transactional vs Transformational Leadership

Transactional and transformational are the two modes of leadership that tend to be compared the most. According to Wikipedia: *Transactional leaders are leaders who exchange tangible rewards for the work and loyalty of followers. Transformational leaders are leaders who engage with followers, focus on higher order, intrinsic needs, and raise consciousness about the significance of specific outcomes and new ways in which those outcomes might be achieved. Transactional leaders tend to be more passive as transformational leaders demonstrate active behaviors that include providing a sense of mission.*

In his 1978 book, *Leadership*, renowned scholar and recipient of a Pulitzer Prize James McGregor Burns introduced the concept of transformational leadership. He defined transformational leadership as a process where "leaders and their followers raise one another to higher levels of morality and motivation."

In 1985 Bernard Bass, in his book, *Leadership and Performance Beyond Expectations*, further refined transformational leadership as:
- A model of integrity and fairness.
- Sets clear goals.
- Has high expectations.
- Encourages others.

- Provides support and recognition.
- Stirs the emotions of people.
- Gets people to look beyond their self-interest.
- Inspires people to reach for the improbable.

Transactional leadership, on the other hand, focuses on organizational structure, managerial hierarchy and rules, directives, executive orders, or whatever one choose to call them. They have no desire to develop, evolve or grow. They endorse compliance through both rewards and punishments and look to keep things the same. Transactional leaders focus on their staff's performance to find faults and deviations. The other side of the transactional leadership coin involves the exchange.

According to Bass and Riggio, transformational leaders, when contrasted with transactional leaders, "help followers develop into leaders by responding to the individual follower's needs. This is typically accomplished by empowering them and by aligning the objectives and goals of the individual followers, the leader, the group, and the larger organization."[3] In this model of transformational Leadership, *alignment* is the key concept. Another term for this could be "parallel programming." It's important to note that Bass and Riggio base much of their work in articulating transformational leadership on the original work of Burns and his description in 1978.

One of the boldest experiments in corporate leadership distribution comes from Zappos.com and the introduction of Holacracy®. Holacracy® is a method of decentralized management and organizational governance developed by

---

[3] Bernard M. Bass and Ronald E. Riggio, *Transformational Leadership*, 2nd ed. (Mahwah, N.J.: L. Erlbaum Associates, 2006).

HolacracyOne. CEO Tony Hsieh introduced the concept to Zappos.com. The purpose is to encourage collaboration, self-governance, and to free employees to make critical decisions. Despite criticism of this approach, Hsieh has said his biggest mistake was not implementing Holacracy® earlier in the company life.

With transformational strategies we can create leadership at every level by:

- Transforming ourselves
- Transforming others
- Creating a perpetual motion machine of leadership where one person transforms another

To begin transforming yourself, you can begin to identify your own personal strengths; you can set intentions, and you can practice the principles of emotional intelligence, mindfulness and positive affirmation. Transforming ourselves requires taking a personal inventory and moving forward from mistakes, seeing even failure as an opportunity for feedback.

Transactional leadership engages theoretical management strategies such as conducting a staff meeting. For example: You bring everyone in, have them sit in a round circle, have them all identify a problem which is frustrating to them, and then try to brainstorm solutions to those problems. Unfortunately, all of the energy of this group is focused on what's wrong and fails to pay attention to what's right.

The opposite of this is the transformational approach: Instead of talking about what's wrong, each person identifies one thing that's right in the company today and one thing that's right with their fellow employees today.

Today is your starting point in mastering a new approach to leadership. And that is to begin with understanding your own strengths. Strength-based management and leadership is centered on finding and refining the strengths of an individual and of a team. Imagine that you are the coach of a baseball team. Each of your players was selected to be on the team because of a certain talent or strength they have. If you have a player that is great at throwing a 95-mph fastball but not so talented at catching the ball, would you put him at shortstop or even behind the plate, catching? Why would you? To "work" on his weaknesses? I'm sure you agree this is crazy. If you think about it though, this is exactly what traditional management/leadership does. I strongly encourage you to find your strengths and allow or help others to find theirs as well. That is what a true team player does and what a true team is. Each member has an assigned strength-based position.

In a broader perspective, leadership is not about becoming something as much as it is about utilizing something. In life, we all have strengths and resources. By taking an inventory of your strengths you are already leading, thus ending the never-ending problem of not being ready for a leadership role. You transcend the moment to be a leader right now, right here, as you read these pages.

In Viral Leadership the key to effective leadership is sharing our intention and vision with others. This creates buy-in as others adapt our ideas as their own. On a practical level this can often be accomplished in the hiring process. Rather than approaching the interview as a chance to grade skills or traits of potential new hires, use this opportunity to share vision and intention and gain-buy in. Those candidates who buy the most are the ones to keep. Skills may be learned, traits can be developed, but buy-in will produce enthusiastic workers who grow a business.

Have you ever watched a street performer? Let's say there is a magician in downtown Las Vegas or a juggler in Amsterdam or a dancer in Buenos Aries. As they begin their performance, they are the only leader. But as soon as just one person stops to watch, and the performer engages them in the act, others will stop to watch and enjoy. With this buy-in momentum others want to be involved and as they line up to clap, participate, dance or be involved, the crowd can grow and grow. What is happening here is that the performer gains buy-in from every spectator. A skilled street performer knows the dynamics of leadership – and involvement and inclusion. They know how to parlay this into not only a profitable night, but sometimes a profitable career. Rod Stewart is a singer who did this by starting on the streets and eventually selling 100 million albums. Robin Williams worked the streets by creating a perpetual motion machine of involvement that began with his street performances as a mime and ended with multiple academy awards.

Viral Leaders spread leadership. They create involvement, they mentor others and they look for leadership at every level. The CEO who has an open door is, in my opinion, far more likely to build a successful organization than the CEO who has a gatekeeper and only sees the highest levels of management.

CHAPTER TWELVE

Lessons in Viral Leadership from Entertainment

Being completely dependent on viral success, the entertainment industry personifies the viral model. In creating your own success, there are lessons to be learned by reflecting on what the entertainment industry teaches us. In almost every case of viral success, the Four Quadrants of Viral Leadership are somewhere to be found, and in music, literature, cinema, art or any other form of entertainment the foundations of intention and authenticity are usually glaring. It is the authentic voice in Joni Mitchell's "Both Sides Now" that made this song an anthem for a generation. It is the brute reality of *The Fight Club* that made it not only a best-selling book, but a movie that will endure the test of time.

Creating something awesome does not equate to viral success. The prerequisites for viral success is not necessarily dependent on quality nor even money. Although these two factors do help to a point, they are not golden tickets to viral success. If you want to take the power of Now and create something sustaining, look for elements of the Four Quadrants of Viral Leadership in entertainment success - then replicate that success in your own business. Many cult or viral movies, such as the Blair Witch Project, Napoleon Dynamite, and the classic Rocky Horror Picture Show, were all shot on shoestring budgets with semi-professional or consumer grade equipment. In fact, the Rocky Horror Picture Show, which debuted in 1975, is still running in select theaters across America!

The music business follows this same pattern with songs that are low budget productions or not composed in the conventional style, yet everyone sings them. Even though they may sound awful or may have the most bizarre lyrics, they become huge viral hits. Think of songs like "Ice Ice Baby" by Vanilla Ice, or what I believe may be the worst viral song ever, "Just a Friend", by Biz Markie. His singing is so off key and off beat that for me, it is unlistenable. Everything about this song is just horrible to me. Another off-putting song that defined a generation and became their anthem was "Smells like Teen Spirit", by Nirvana. Everything about this song pretty much goes against the rules of good song writing, musical structuring and performance. I can't even make out the words, let alone understand what he's singing about. Now don't get me wrong. I understand this is "art" and is also a generational thing. Back when I was a young teen, my parents hated "my" music as well. To them, bands like Led Zeppelin and AD/DC were loud, obnoxious and just screamed incomprehensible mumbo-jumbo and, according to them, it was all about sex and drugs! But all this noise was pure, sweet music to my ears!

For me, Jim Morrison and the Doors are the epitome of everything viral. They had Viral Leadership. They were a Viral Team. They were always on the cutting edge of the "now," and they knew how to attract, gain, maintain and grow their fan base. The catalog of hits by the Doors is amazing and has withstood the test of time. What was so impressive is how they all worked together as a team. All their songs were written by The Doors; they all composed and wrote together as a team. They focused on their individual strengths and collaboratively created viral success. Unlike so many other bands, they didn't let their egos or greed get in the way of what they had created. At one point, GM approached them about using "Light My Fire" in a Buick commercial, wanting to change the lyrics to "Come on, Buick, Light My Fire." The multimillion dollar deal was turned down because it was only a 3 to 1 vote, not a 4 and 0. Although the band stuck to their artistic guns, they did however continue to act on their Nows.

One of the keys to The Doors' viral success was that from a business standpoint, they understood their clientele. They were so in touch with what their audience desired and created music that embraced the human experience. These were radical, rapidly changing times and the birth of a new (hippie) generation. The great metaphorical songs they created and performed became the voice of this generation. Twelve years after it was written, Francis Ford Copula chose the song "The End" to be the signature song for his blockbuster movie, "Apocalypse Now." This movie and The Doors' music defined the Vietnam War, along with the unrest of the times. The movie also introduced the legendary Doors to a whole new generation. It is worth noting that The Doors often recorded their music in a rather amateurish style; their final studio album, "L.A. Woman" wasn't even made in a recording studio. They recorded it in their practice room, or in other words, in their garage!

Even the death of Jim Morrison at age 27 did not quell the success of The Doors, from a commercial perspective, and can actually be a lesson to any leader that no matter how skilled, talented, innovative or authentic you are - you must also address your own personal demons. Too many great leaders end up like Morrison, not necessarily dead at age 27, but washed up in their ability to continue to create powerful professional impact as a result of private, personal failures.

In our current day and age, music is also linked to videos, thanks to MTV, and now through the second most accessed search engine in the universe: Youtube.com. I really don't think any song these days has a chance of ever going viral without a video these days. Music videos, and YouTube, have dramatically changed the game. Although the YouTube platform is available to anyone and everyone, there is still a formula for viral sustainability. This is what makes the difference between flash-in-the-pan one-hit wonders and a viral sensation with growth and sustainability.

The song/video, "Gangnam Style" by Korean rapper Psy, went viral on YouTube, becoming the first of its kind to reach over 1 and later 2 billion views. He held this position for over 5 years until it was surpassed by Wiz Khalifa's song, "See You Again", which, as of this writing, has been watched over 3.1 billion times. Yes, Gangnam was a hit, a huge viral hit, but it failed to have sustainable success. Psy didn't build upon the Now or turn that viral success into something bigger and sustainable. Psy is also a great case study in failing to seize the power of Now to create something sustainable. Although educated in America, his previous public comments about the US military came to light with his fame, resulting his public apology and now Psy largely performs only in the East Asian market - one that might be more forgiving of his public political comments than the American audiences who made him rich. Leadership requires personal discipline, and our greatest barrier to long term success can sometimes be ourselves and our own weaknesses.

Let's look at viral success that produces sustainability. In 2013, one of the most successful music videos to date is a song called, "The Fox", or as many know it, "What does the fox say?" I find this song so creatively annoying that I can't help but blast it if it comes on the radio. But, the genius of this little ditty is the sustained success the group has manifested from this song. By taking action at the height of their viralness, Norwegian brothers Vegard and Bard Ylvisaker landed a record deal with Warner Music, a TV show, and if that's not enough, they signed a children's book deal with publishing giants Simon & Schuster! They took their viral success and parlayed their Now into a successful and profitable business.

Books are also big in the world of entertainment viral-ability with over 400,000 books written each year. But which ones become best sellers? The same question may be asked about movies and television. Throughout our modern era literally thousands and thousands of books, songs, movies and TV shows have been created, but only a handful of them have managed to create viral success and sustainable growth. We call these timeless classics and they include titles like Catcher in the Rye, Little Women, The Great Gatsby, all classics. Some movies and TV shows are multi-generational hits as well, like The Wizard of Oz and Star Wars. TV shows like M.A.S.H, Cheers and Friends are all still running in syndication. Characters like vampires and zombies are now going on two centuries of viral awareness.

Business can learn a lot from the entertainment industry about Viral Leadership. "Build it and they will come," only works in Hollywood movies. In real life, creating something awesome does not necessarily equate to viral success. What makes an entertainment product viral? This is what business leaders can inquire from the entertainment industry.

A song become a viral smash hit not necessarily because it is good in the conventional sense, but rather, because people can relate to it in one way or another. A catchy beat helps, but it is the meaning and/or emotion of the song that people connect with. It can be a heartwarming happy in love feeling, a broken heart emotion or a get up and boogie response. If it can connect with the masses, it can become viral. In other words – authenticity. This is what The Doors were so good at; they heard, defined, connected with and became one with their audience.

Songs, books, movies, television show became smash hits because everyone can relate to them in one way or another. When people read, hear or see a metaphor, the subconscious mind attaches to it the meaning most important to them. Many of the components of these hits are metaphorical or abstract. What does a song, a book, movie or TV show mean? It means whatever the person thinks it means. A good example of this is Jimmy Webb's "MacArthur Park", recorded by such stars as Frank Sinatra, Tony Bennett, Donna Summer, The Four Tops and, most recently, Carrie Underwood. Led Zeppelin's "Kashmir" is another song with obscure lyrics that have endless metaphors. Here are a few lines:

*Oh, let the sun beat down upon my face, and
  stars fill my dream
I'm a traveler of both time and space, to be
  where I have been
To sit with elders of the gentle race, this
  world has seldom seen
They talk of days for which they sit and
  wait, all will be revealed*

*Oh, pilot of the storm who leaves no trace, like
  sorts inside a dream
Leave the path that led me to that place,
  Yellow desert stream
Like Shangri-La beneath the summer
  moon, I will return again
As the dust that floats finds you, we're
  moving through Kashmir*

So, for businesses who want viral success, it's important to allow the customer or the team attach the meaning that is most important to them. In my marketing of educational programs, I started using the tagline, "Continuing Education Courses with Meaning." I never say what the meaning is (to me). I leave it unanswered. Everyone who comes across my marketing and considers the courses have to look inside themselves to decide what the meaning is to them. For some, it's a fancy certification. For others, it's a sense of accomplishment. For others, practical answers. The answer is always there. The outcome of this simple adjustment: sales up over 20% within the first year following adapting this tagline.

Here are the 5 key strategies, or takeaways you can learn from the entertainment industry, so you can become a smash hit and go viral as well:

- Be genuine and do what you do because it's your passion.
- Create a strength-based team and let your team be a team.
- Know your audience and give them what they want, rather than telling them what they want.
- Act upon the Now and keep creating new "Nows".
- Having faith and resilience are a must.

CHAPTER THIRTEEN

Develop your Decisiveness

The saying goes, "Life is full of regrets." The business world is littered with stories of missed opportunities. Ronald Wayne co-founded Apple Computers with Steve Jobs and Steve Wozniak. He gave up his 10% stake early on for $800 because he was purchasing a house and worried about his personal credit liability. That 10% stake would be worth a cool $35 *billion* dollars today. And of course, Decca Records passed on the Beatles in 1962, letting much smaller EMI dominate the music of the 1960s.

Do you remember Borders bookstores? In 2003, over 1,249 stores dotted the American landscape. By 2011, they declared bankruptcy. Procrastination in the digital age means that opportunity will pass you like a 220 mph Lamborghini on the highway of life. Borders had a huge retail footprint, but it was saddled with long-term debt and longer-term leases. These obligations made it impossible at that time to navigate the emergence of digital transformation. They farmed out their internet sales channel to Amazon and did not even launch a website until 2008. What followed was an even worse string of bad decisions. They chose to keep stocking their stores with DVDs and CDs *after* consumers' trends had made a serious right turn to digital media. Leadership decisions also never fully embraced the E-reader, leaving the Kindle to dominate the market. During the same period that Borders failed to embrace the E-reader, Amazon sold 43.7 million of the Kindle devices. Barnes and Noble fully embraced the NOOK E-reader and it thrives as a competitor to the Kindle.

The simple reason for Borders' failure is that Amazon put them out of business. But Barnes and Noble survived. Books-A-Million survived and currently operates 260 stores. Half Price Books Survived. Hudson News survived, as did many others. To contrast those that have endured, Books-A-Million opened their website in 1998, a full ten years before Borders even tried.

Developing your decisiveness is key to seizing the power of Now and stepping into the future. Those who take action reap rewards and, in an era where shift happens quickly, reflective urgency is key. Reactive urgency is simply acting too quickly without critical thought. This leads to ignoring the importance of intention and keeping the vision in view. Many companies have been guilty of reactive urgency. Launching a new product, for example, without any relationship to its core values or critical thinking leads to disaster. Attempting to jump onto the billion-dollar bottled water bandwagon, Coors Brewing Company introduced *Coors Rocky Mountain Sparkling Water*. This was their first non-alcoholic beverage since the prohibition era and was a case of reactive urgency. There is also deliberative non-urgency, where a company deliberates the benefits of action for such a long time that when they finally do act, it's too little, too late. Borders, finally putting up a website, 10 years after every single other book retailer had done, so demonstrated the prime example of deliberative non-urgency.

Reflective Urgency, on the other hand, is based on knowing one's intentions, setting and evaluating one's goals and taking actions that produce transformation. Reflective urgency comes from understanding that extreme deviations from core products, values or industry trends also leads to disaster. Asking fundamental questions of yourself can also help develop reflective urgency. "What are my intentions?" and "Am I reflecting the strengths of my team in my decisions?" These types of questions will help generate reflective urgency, gaining foresight for the completion of the goals. This differs from what we commonly refer to as "gut instinct." This primitive trait is an evolutionary strategy that helped us recognize friend or foe. Gut feelings are a holdover of tribal loyalty development. Gut instinct is emotional response. As a therapist, my biggest battle over the years has been with clients I had to convince that feelings are not the same things as facts. As a professor, I can attest that intuition is a decision-making reflex that cannot replace reflective urgency skill development.

Without a doubt, the most effective way to develop the skill of reflective urgency is silence. In silence we can listen, not only to the words of others on our team, but we can also sort through the stream of information, often with conflicting messages, that barrage our computer monitors and smart phones each day. I have tracked the ever-increasing messages and pieces of information that come to me each day. I get barraged with about 600 personal messages per day, including emails, social media accounts, text messages, etc.

This does not include the countless and meaningless ads we all get (estimated as up to as many as 4000 per day). Now add the 10s of thousands of ponderous thoughts that are mulling around in our own head each day – many of which, research shows, are negative thoughts. Many people feel a sense of overload from all this information and stimuli and the trend lately has been to "unplug". But even while on vacation many people stay in touch with these messages; depending on your online activity while on vacation, you may even get more messages, ads, and mental demands!

Meditation to "clear one's thoughts" has been advocated, but it has been my experience that the number one reason people can't get into the practice of meditation is that they find it impossible to still their thoughts. And herein lies the problem: A fish swims in water. It does not know it swims in water because it is always in water. It has never been out of water. People are like fish but instead of swimming in water people swim in thoughts. To demand a fish to get out of the water is as unnatural as a person getting "out" of their thoughts.

The silence of reflective urgency is not detachment, it is about two skills. First, staying in the moment, which is why mindfulness meditation has become the most popular form of meditation in America. It does not demand we get out of the metaphorical water but rather that we just let a thought be a thought. The key in mindfulness meditation is not in not thinking but in not following a thought and projecting into the future. The second skill is listening without judgement. I am not talking about the judgement of whether this is good or bad, or the judgement of other people here, but rather the judgement that says a thought, feeling or sensation needs an immediate response. Although a fish will always be in water, if you see a Koi pond in the evening the fish are very still. They are still in water but appear almost motionless. By practicing ways to not be judgmental, we can let a thought just be a thought, and an emotion just be an emotion.

Years ago, I was driving with my teenage son from Tulsa to Wichita. It is a long and boring 3-hour drive. We planned to eat healthy food at our favorite Thai restaurant, once we arrived in Wichita. We were about 80 miles from our destination when I stopped for gas at the turnpike service center. While filling the tank, my son jumped out of the car and said he was going to get a burger. I asked him why, since he knew we would be at the Thai restaurant in a little over an hour. He said, "Don't worry Dad, I'm a growing boy, I can eat twice." Our goal at that time if you recall, was to eat healthy, and, McDonalds just didn't seem compatible with our present goal. So, I said to him, "Okay, if you must, but you are being judgmental."

"Judgmental?"

"Yes, judgmental. You have noticed your hunger and you have judged it, coming the conclusion you must make it go away now, even if it means eating something that is not healthy." I said.

"How is that judgmental? I am hungry now and I'm going to get a burger" he said.

"I did not tell you not to. I was just pointing out that you are judging your hunger rather than just letting your hunger be hunger."

"What is that supposed to mean?" he asked with irritation.

"It means that you have not let hunger just be hunger. It's a part of our digestive process and something that is neither good nor bad, but just is."

Once I finished pumping gas and was back in my car, my son soon opened his door and empty-handedly jumped into the car. I asked him what happened to the burger. He said, "Just drive. I'll wait until we get to Wichita." I am pretty sure he muttered something under his breath about having a psychotherapist for a dad and then put on his headphones.

How do we listen without judgement? It is really all about practicing acceptance. What follows is a short dissertation I wrote to help those practicing reflective urgency to practice acceptance:

THE PARADOX...is that when something is ACCEPTED as just being what it is, it then holds no POWER. Depression, loneliness, hunger, fear or even withdrawal become unimportant when accepted.

When it becomes unimportant, it becomes just...what is.

It is something experienced, rather than something I fight or hate, or something I am restricted by or obsessed with. I can find FREEDOM from suffering.

Depression is not a problem. Hunger is not a problem. Withdrawal is not a problem. Loneliness is not a problem. It is only a problem if I make it one. These things let me know I am a Human Being NOT a human doing.

Happiness would suck if life had no depression.

Security would suck if we had no sense of fear to put it in perspective.

Difficult times and experiences are a part of any valued path. Difficulty and even pain are not to be avoided if one wants a truly meaningful life. They are simply things to accept, because in acceptance…we give no power to control, and it becomes the pathway to being:

A FULL HUMAN BEING PARTICIPATING FULLY IN LIFE

The Heart of Reflective Urgency is Intention

Remember the importance of intention in the previous chapters? In reflective urgency, we are taking decisive action, but what is it reflecting? It is reflecting our intentions. It is reflecting our why.

Why do we sell, or why do we build, or why do we do our work? In his book, *Start with Why*, author Simon Sinek turns around our understanding of good marketing and moves the reader from the features and benefits of a product or service to the why of the product or service. He shares the success story of Apple in defining themselves not by how they build computers or what they build, but rather by why they build: To be innovative.

He also gives the example of a company that, despite having the necessary resources, failed to make a profit. That company is TiVo. They prided themselves on building the best products on the market. The problem with that is that they never differentiated themselves from the clones who make similar products. TiVo loaded us up with what they built, but not the why. Sinek seems to conclude that if they had lead with the why, they would have marketed as a company who lets you have total control over your life.

In the case of reflective urgency, the why really matters. It lets you take action in the moment, while fulfilling your intention. I sold Hondas and Nissans when I was an undergraduate. As I gravitated toward counseling and psychology I began to envision myself as a "car counselor." I shifted from the idea of selling cars because it was my job, to one of helping people find the right car for their family. I found car sales to be a way for me to practice my intention of being a good therapist before I had the chance to do actual counseling. The results were amazing! I began to see every customer as someone I could help. Once I shifted my thinking, I ended up each month as the highest grossing salesman. Kamran, who was hired at the same time I was, sold cars to make money. He soon became the top salesperson on the team. On the average he would sell twice as many cars as anyone else. I, however, made more money than the rest of the sales staff including Kamran. It was the <u>why</u> that created my intention.

Here are 7 things to reflect on when making decisions:
- Why does it matter?
- Why do we care?
- Why do we lead?
- Why do we succeed?
- Why do we do what we do?
- Why will this engage others?
- Why is the team involved?

These questions will help you to master your intentions and reflect quickly on the decisions that must be made. After defining one's <u>why</u>, we must next look at <u>what</u> and <u>how</u>. This is most effectively enhanced by the <u>why</u> of intention. There are many other questions that leaders can ask to help take decisive action. They include questions such as:
- What is the meaning to the stakeholders created by a product or action?
- What is the context of the decision?

- How does the action impact the vision of the organization?
- How does the project contribute to community at every level?

Trust Yourself

The heart of developing decisiveness is learning to trust yourself. For new leaders in positions where their actions will be judged against the performance of others, maintaining the status quo is a powerful temptation. But no action *is* an action - an action that most often results in the opposite of what one desired. It is also the opposite of what it means to harness Viral Leadership.

Katrina Lake was told by her professors at Harvard Business School that her idea for an online clothing retailer was an "inventory nightmare" and she quotes one venture capitalist as saying, "I just don't understand why anyone would want anything like this!" But Lake proved them all wrong when Stitch Fix posted 2016 revenue of $730 Million, and her 2017 revenue was almost $1 Billion dollars. How did she do it? By trusting in herself, her vision and the science behind online clothing sales.

Her business is not unique; selling clothing is a crowded field, and many people have a dislike for online clothes shopping. But Lake's idea was to leverage the power of analytics and couple it with a human touch to create loyal customers who would pay top dollar for clothing curated by both real life designers and powerful algorithms. The business she created, Stich Fix, is as much a technology company as it is a retailer or clothier, and her use of data science to know the customer, build loyalty, and create viral enthusiasm is powerful.

Lake crafted the idea while contrasting the death of brick-and-mortar Blockbuster and the growth of online movie provider Netflix. Eric Colson from Netflix joined her team as Chief Algorithms Officer in 2012 and today Stich Fix employees, data scientists, and real-life fashion consultants create a unique desire among consumers for products. Stitch Fox now designs its own brand, Hybrid Designs, to meet the desires and demands of customers whose secret preferences are now being revealed by the algorithm. This company is as much a futuristic data science company as it is a retailer - and it now has the revenue to prove the nay-sayers wrong because, at its core, Katrina Lake believed in both science and herself.

Many long-term leaders frequently fail to trust themselves. They perhaps feel they got lucky before and do not want to break their winning streak. By doing something new or harnessing a viral moment, they begin to cultivate a "scarcity" mentality, believing that success is infrequent and should be preserved and rationed rather than continuously pursued.

Back in the 1980s, Stewart Smalley, a character on Saturday Night Live, used to sit in front of the mirror and say, "I'm good enough, I'm smart enough, and doggone it, people like me." That was his affirmation to himself. It was a Saturday Night Live skit that really spoofed self-help programs and the whole affirmation movement. I love affirmations. I think that they can be a tool in Positive Psychology. I think that Stewart Smalley may have been funny, but Stewart Smalley got it correct. Affirmations, when used well, are extremely effective.

The reason why is simple: Anybody who's been practicing Cognitive Behavioral Therapy knows that we need to counter cognitive errors. The most effective way to counter cognitive errors is with the truth, and those truths can become affirmations. Outside of any Twelve-Step meeting, you'll see cars with bumper stickers reading, "Just for Today," or "One Day at a Time." Those are affirmations. Those affirmations have become one of the most important elements of the success of Twelve-Step programs. Why? Because they are effective counters to cognitive errors.

At the current time, our cultural awareness of the value of affirmations has moved beyond Stewart Smalley and now focuses on the Law of Attraction. You may recognize some of these phrases: *"Like attracts like"* or *"Birds of a feather flock together."* In his book, *The Power of I Am and the Law of Attraction*, my co-author RJ Banks states: *"We are and attract into our lives what we choose to think, say, and believe about ourselves and our perceived reality."* These are examples of affirmations or positive self-talk.

Similarly, a lot of the leaders I train are familiar with the power of the Word from their study of the biblical creation account. It begins, of course, in Genesis with God speaking. This creation story is reflected both in Christian tradition as well as the stories of other cultures. In Buddhism, one aspect of the Eightfold Path called the Sama Vaca is often translated to English as Right Speech. The more accurate rendering is Wise Speech, or even Skillful Speech, which hopefully suggests speech that is acquired through practice.

The Power of Affirmations

Not only does our culture, whether in Saturday Night Live, books and movies about the Law of Attraction, or religious scriptures, talk about the power of the spoken word, philosophers and metaphysicians in the past hundred years have written profoundly on this subject. Charles Haanel, who is an industrialist and the founder of the St. Louis Post Dispatch Newspaper, wrote these words, *"Thought is energy. Active thought is active energy. Concentrated thought is a concentrated energy. Thought concentrated on a definite purpose becomes power."*[4]

William Walker Atkinson, a metaphysician and philosopher from the early 1900s, wrote the best way to overcome undesirable or negative thoughts and feelings is to cultivate the positive ones.[5]

In the early '60s, Earl Nightingale was awarded the first Gold Record for his spoken word album, *The Strangest Secret*. His message was: *"We become what we think about most of the time."*

How Do We Use Affirmations?

Of course, affirmations can be repeated daily, like a rosary, but there are many other ways to use affirmations.

None of my clients ever leave my office without this set of instructions: I give them a dry-erase marker, telling them to take this dry-erase marker home and write a positive

---

[4] Charles F. Haanel, *The Master Key System in Twenty-Four Parts with Questionnaire and Glossary* (Saint Louis, Mo.: 1919).

[5] William Walker Atkinson and Harry Houdini Collection (Library of Congress), *Thought Vibration, or, the Law of Attraction in the Thought World* (Chicago, U.S.A.: Library Shelf, 1910).

affirmation on their bathroom mirror. That way, the first thing they see in the morning, the last thing they see at night and something they see repeatedly throughout the day is the counter to their cognitive error staring back at them in their own handwriting. This can become a powerful technique and a simple method for helping our clients make change. If you don't have a drawer full of dry-erase markers, go buy them in bulk from an office supply store. I guarantee you even if they don't believe it when they wrote it, they will test the affirmation to find if it's true. It will almost always result in dramatic change.

RJ Banks offers his clients his "My Morning Affirmations", a list of extremely effective "I Am" affirmations to start one's day with. They are:

- I Am Happy
- I Am Healthy
- I Am Wealthy
- I Am Loved
- I Am Secure
- I Am Worthy
- I Am Forgiving
- I Am Forgiven
- I Am Blessed
- I Am Grateful
- I Am Beautiful
- I Am Confident
- I Am Courageous
- I Am Excited About Today

I also ask my coaching clients to put their affirmations on a screensaver on their computer as well. Anyone can create their own screen saver in about two minutes. Affirmations can be shared as a Facebook status. It's amazing how the social reinforcement, the "likes" that a client receives in response to posting a positive affirmation, can make that affirmation come alive. Interestingly, there's a ton of research showing that that's true.[6] The *likes* are a very important part of psychological phenomena.

With such great advancements in technology, audio affirmations programs have become extremely popular. Whether it be while driving, walking, exercising, meditating or whatever the situation, people can listen to their audio affirmations programs anytime they desire.

---

[6] C. L. Toma and J. T. Hancock, "Self-Affirmation Underlies Facebook Use," *Pers Soc Psychol Bull* 39, no. 3 (2013).

EPILOGUE

The Result is Lasting Transformation in Business

CHAPTER FOURTEEN

Activating the Power of Now

Peter Drucker famously said, *"The best way to predict the future is to create it."* By focusing on the potential for Viral Leadership you are creating the future by harnessing the power of Now. Drucker also said, *"Long-range planning does not deal with future decisions, but with the future of present decisions."* Viral Leadership is important because it is the form of leadership most likely to frame decisions as creating the future and it is the form of leadership that focuses on futurity.

In his book, *Management: Tasks, Practices, and Responsibilities,* Drucker writes: "*Strategic planning does not deal with future decisions. It deals with the futurity of present decisions. Decisions only exist in the present. The question that faces the strategic decision-maker is not what his organization should do tomorrow. It is, 'What do we have to do today to be ready for an uncertain tomorrow?' The question is not what will happen in the future. It is, 'What futurity do we have to build into our present thinking and doing, what time spans do we have to consider, and how do we use this information to make a rational decision now?'*"

Viral Leadership is the approach to leadership that makes actionable the idea that decisions only exist in the present. There are no such things as "future decisions" to be made. How many times have you been in a meeting where something was tabled so that "future decisions could be made?" But we don't know what the future holds. If anyone could predict the future with certainty they would be ruler of the world! To focus on future decisions, is to miss the power of Now. Today creates the future. Viral Leadership understands that. The outcome of our Now decisions lets us flow with the unlimited possibilities that will emerge. As leadership transforms others and contributions are added, resources become generated and viral excitement creates now opportunities.

Business is one of the most creative, ingenious and resourceful endeavors known to mankind. Yes, art, music, and literature are creative, but business changes mankind in a different way. Ancient and modern manmade wonders of the world such as the Great Pyramid of Giza, the Great Wall of China, Stonehenge etc., are all awe-inspiring, but Microsoft, Walmart, and Toyota Motor company are all equally as amazing.

The Japanese construction company Kongo Gumi Co. has been in business since 578 AD. It has been family owned and operated continuously for over 1400 years. They are still in business to this day! The Royal Mint in the UK has been in business for over 1150 years. In America, there are several businesses over 200 years old. There is a pretty good chance while you are reading this book that you are wearing a Brooks Brothers shirt, or at least have one in your closet. They have been filling our closets for over 200 years. In 1795, Jacob

Beam created and sold his first barrel of whiskey. The Colgate toothpaste hit the shelves in 1873 but the company had been in business selling soap and candles since 1806. According to their website, that company today has more than $15 billion and sells its products in over 200 countries and territories worldwide.

The foundation of any successful company's longevity can almost always be traced to an explosive enthusiasm that captured the moment. Today we call these "a-ha" moments. Building upon this initial enthusiasm through effective leadership, one can transform society and create something sustaining. This is the very nature of Viral Leadership. Viral Leadership is necessary because it transforms people and cultures. Can you imagine how life would be entirely different if Microsoft had never existed? Without Microsoft we would largely be using bucket-specific applications rather than cross-platform user experiences. Everything would be different. From the personal PC that most everyone on the planet uses today, to the entire foundations of business communications, product development and how people interact, Microsoft plays a major role in everyone's daily life. Would you even have the same career, doing what you do, if Microsoft never existed?

Viral Leadership is your pathway to seizing the moment, and potentially impacting billions of people with something that changes every aspect of life. We can't go any further in our discussion about life-changing Viral Leadership without discussing Facebook. Facebook is clearly the epitome of modern day viral impact and a legacy of changing lives. History will look back at the profound nature of Facebook, perhaps with goodwill or perhaps with harsh judgment.

Either way, there can be no doubt how Zuckerberg's creation has impacted just about everything in our modern culture, from election results on a global level to its influence on the family. In the U.K., 33% of divorce petitions contained the word "Facebook". Facebook has also disrupted the way small business advertises. It has changed communication and broken the monopoly email once held over personal communications while memes have become a form of moral police.

These are real results that change humanity. History will judge which of these changed humanity for the better and which contributed to our downfall. Make no mistake, modern companies, antique companies, and historic companies have all altered the course of mankind forever. The results are profound. Yes, Shakespeare changed the English language. Picasso's *Guernica* provoked a visceral response to war, an impression that has lasted decades.

One of the most prolific legacies of our modern times is that of Standard Oil and the family name behind it - The Rockefellers. Their wealth, influence and impact persist to this day, with political implications at every level for over a century. The legacy of Standard Oil defines the past century of business structure and organization and the antitrust laws which affect current businesses to this day. Communities and people numbering in the millions have been directly impacted by the creation of Standard Oil - in both positive and negative ways.

John D. Rockefeller (the founder of Standard Oil) was a Viral Leader. His motto was to always try to turn every disaster into an opportunity. He even succeeded at this when the Supreme Court broke his monopoly in 1911. Rockefeller is also quoted as saying, ""I would rather earn 1% off 100 people's efforts than 100% of my own efforts." And while there is certainly a cynical way of interpreting this quote the essence of Viral Leadership is the ability to create critical mass. Viral Leadership leverages success.

Viral Leadership is important because it produces true freedom. It frees a leader from being the sole source of power and from being reliant on their own, limited resources. The truth is, we only know what we know, and even though some of us are smart and know a lot, the collective knowledge base from manager, employees, customers, and the community are unleashed to transform business when Viral Leadership is applied.

Henry Ford understood the power of Viral Leadership and how a collaborative think tank is much more creative than the single-minded ego. "I have a row of electric push buttons on my desk", he said, "and by pushing the right button, I can summon to my aid men who can answer any question I desire to ask concerning the business to which I am devoting most of my efforts." By creating his "Master Mind" group, the Ford legacy became what it is today. His invention of the Model T automobile in 1908 has had an impact on every person on the planet. Henry Ford and his Master Mind team have created, developed and improved the motor vehicle to what it is today and hold several patents within the automobile manufacturing industry.

One of the foremost appeals of Viral Leadership is that it is exciting; the potential to impact so many lives in a positive way allows us to find joy in what we do. One can see beyond the drudgery of today's tasks and create a vision for the future. The excitement of viral potential unleashes Now intentions and gives way to new thoughts, new relationships and new ways of living. The popular restaurant chain, Benihana, gained its success by jumping on a Now opportunity and has become the worldwide leader in tableside teppanyaki restaurants. With the business failing and just days before closing for good, the owner of a small coffee shop in Tokyo carelessly left the door from the kitchen to the dining room propped open. On this day, a small group of local businessmen stopped in for lunch. With the door to the kitchen propped open, the customers could see the cooks hard at work. The businessmen were amazed and highly entertained by the impromptu cooking show they then witnessed. They were astounded and amazed at the razzle dazzle knife skills these modern-day samurais possessed.

The very next day this same group of businessmen returned for yet another show. Only on this day, they brought a larger group of colleagues with them to witness and enjoy this astonishing culinary art experience. The following day, the dining room was filled with customers and the crowd demanded the grill be brought out into the dining room. The rest, as they say, is history.

I have always said that ultimately, the purpose of leadership is happiness and Viral Leadership provides a fast-track to human happiness. We want to be happy at work and when an enthused team begins working together to capture the moment and create something of meaning, the workplace is a happy place. When I come home from work happy, the happiness exudes to my family, and life is just better for all of us. Even my dog, Wang Cai, is happy when I am happy. Viral Leadership is a source of happiness and that happiness can, in and of itself, become transformational and sustaining.

Do you want to be a Viral Leader? Then take the first step. Set an intention. Set the intention to be your best and to be observant and to take action.

VIRAL LEADERSHIP

WITH DR. RICHARD NONGARD

Keynote Speaker and Corporate Training

Seize the power of Now to create lasting transformation in business. Proven keys for activating leadership across every organization.

Dr. Richard Nongard is an experienced speaker who is engaging, easy going, and shares actionable strategies for sales professionals, leadership teams, executives, and front-line personnel. He is passionate about helping everyone uncover leadership potential and use it to create lasting change.

Call Richard at (918) 236-6116 to reserve your dates.

www.ingramcontent.com/pod-product-compliance
Lightning Source LLC
Chambersburg PA
CBHW020655220526
45464CB00001B/450